Clyde Steamers

GLORY DAYS

Brian Patton

Ian Allan PUBLISHING

A sunset view of the *Queen Mary* at Wemyss Bay in 1977. *Dr Alastair C. Harper*

Front cover:
The last turbine steamer to be built for the CSPC, the *Marchioness of Graham* of 1936, approaches Brodick in 1957, well laden with cars. *D. Cox, courtesy Mrs J. Cox and the Isle of Arran Heritage Museum*

Back cover:
The *Duchess of Hamilton* (1932) sets off from Keppel for Campbeltown on a June Sunday in 1969. *Author*

Title page:
The *Queen Mary II* at Wemyss Bay in June 1973, during her first year in Caledonian MacBrayne colours. *Author*

CONTENTS

*For Aunt Margaret,
who has known these ships so well*

First published 2003

ISBN 0 7110 2925 3

Published by Ian Allan Publishing

an imprint of Ian Allan Publishing Ltd, Hersham, Surrey KT12 4RG. Printed by Ian Allan Printing Ltd, Hersham, Surrey KT12 4RG.

Code: 0307/B1

INTRODUCTION

In a history of 190 years, it is hard to date exactly the glory days of the Clyde steamers. However, it seemed that the century between 1877 and 1977 would form a convenient focus for this book. The former year saw the real beginning of pleasure cruising on the Firth of Clyde, with a ship whose on-board facilities would attract those who might not otherwise be persuaded to take a day's sail on the water, on which the cruise itself was just as important as the destination. The latter marked the end of commercial cruising by steamer, with the withdrawal of the *Queen Mary*. In the intervening century, the steamers endeared themselves to thousands — to the commuters glad to be safely home again in Dunoon or Rothesay on a winter's night, to the tourists from outwith Scotland marvelling at the scenery and the services, to the thousands of Glasgow folk escaping downriver at the Fair, to the locals who still depend on the Clyde ferries to take them about their daily business, to all those for whom a day trip to Inveraray on board the *Duchess of Montrose* is still a cherished memory. For all of these, it is hoped that this selection will revive memories of the glory days and bring as much pleasure as it has given me to compile.

Compilation would not have been possible without the generous help of a great many people, and I should like to thank these for assistance so willingly given:

Mrs V. Boa (Inverclyde Museums); Ms B. Cole (National Railway Museum); Mrs J. Cox, Eaglesham; John Edgington, York; Stuart Gough, Brodick; Robert Grieves, Paisley; Dr Alastair C. Harper, Glasgow; Bruce A. Jenkins, Kent; Martin Jenkins, Walton-on-Thames (OnLine Video Archives); Roger Jones, Horsham; Douglas McGowan, Cheltenham; Ian Maclagan, Rothesay; Tom McGhie (Caledonian Railway Association); Ms D. Paul (Science Museum, London); Jimmy Poole, Gillingham (World Ship Society); Stuart Rankin, Paisley; David Whiteside, Carlisle (World Ship Society); also the staff of the Glasgow Room, the Mitchell Library, Glasgow, and of the Scottish Records Office, West Register House, Edinburgh, and the committee of the Isle of Arran Heritage Museum, Brodick.

Brian Patton
Foulden, Berwickshire
March 2003

◄ **'Steaming up the Firth'.** Looking ahead towards Strone and the Holy Loch from the port sponson of the *Mercury* (1934). *Author's collection*

1. THE CLYDE IN 1877

At the beginning of 1877 there were 35 steamers available for service on the Clyde, though only a small proportion of these would have been running in winter. As many paddle steamers had been purchased for use as blockade-runners in the early 1860s, the average age of the fleet was low, at 13.2 years. Despite this, almost all the steamers were old-fashioned in design, many being directly based on the first vessels which had plied from 1812, and all but one (the *Kintyre*) were paddle steamers. Most were flush-decked, all accommodation being below main-deck level and thus somewhat cramped and claustrophobic. Sponson houses on either side of the large paddle boxes provided room for a galley — with a chimney painted in the colour scheme of the steamer's funnel — and primitive lavatory facilities. Seven ships of an improved design

had a raised quarter deck, in which the after deck was raised to the level of the main rail, allowing a more commodious cabin below, but only four had deck saloons. When a meal service was provided, it was served at one sitting in the after cabin and no choice of dishes was available. Alcohol was plentiful and cheap.

The captain, who in many cases owned the ship, acted as purser and often presided at table in addition, assisted by a single steward. He may have worn a nautical cap as a sign of rank, though many captains preferred a felt hat or, for special occasions, a top hat. Crew members might have worn a jersey with the ship's name emblazoned on it but otherwise had little in the way of uniform. Bearing in mind that fairly small ships might be carrying up to 1,000 people, there would be close contact with fellow passengers, which became a major

A scene on a Glasgow Fair Saturday at Rothesay between 1884 and 1889, as seen from a house in Victoria Street. The esplanade and gardens (laid out in 1872) are still fairly quiet, but the pier is black with people and many more are about to disembark from the *Lancelot* from Wemyss Bay. On Fair Saturday 1883, 16,000 people left Glasgow for the coast on 20 steamers between 6am and mid-day, and of course this figure does not take account of those who travelled by rail to Wemyss Bay or Greenock. *McLean Museum & Art Gallery*

problem when these fellow passengers had been indulging in a few drinks. Few steamers had facilities to commend them to the passenger. They were simply a very basic means of conveyance. However, it was probably the personal aspect of this kind of service which later led many people to view the railway companies as large, impersonal corporations.

Older steamers were powered by the 'steeple' engine, the design of which dated back to 1818. Newer ships had a diagonal engine with a single crank, the movement of which imparted a distinct surging motion to the ship, and seated passengers could be seen to sway back and forth in time to the pulse of the engine. On a longer trip, this could become wearing. A very few steamers had oscillating engines, which avoided this problem at the expense of higher consumption of coal and increased space in the engine room. All these types of engine were inefficient, consuming copious quantities of coal, much of which went straight up the funnel in the form of unburned particles, immediately to fall again onto the deck below. Many illustrations, clearly taken on a fine day, show a forest of umbrellas on the after deck, as passengers tried to protect themselves from this hail. The engine room was normally completely enclosed, and the traditional excuse of husbands on Clyde steamers, that they were 'going down to see the engines' (when in fact they were making for the bar), originated at a later date!

The only exception to the above was Hutcheson's *Iona* (1864), which provided a much higher standard of comfort and service, as befitted a ship which was the preferred means of travel to the West Highlands for wealthy English tourists and landowners *en route* to their estates in late July and August.

Fares were generally low, and a return trip to Rothesay from Glasgow by steamers such as the *Athole* would therefore have cost about 1s 6d in the cabin and 1s in steerage. A family of two adults and two children travelling cabin would have paid 4s 6d for a day's outing, at a time when £1 10s would have been accounted a fair wage. Probably because of the level of fares, Clyde steamers were not particularly profitable, despite the crowds carried at busy times. Very often steamers were not insured, to save on the premiums.

Although only the North British Railway actually operated steamers, and only in a small way, the influence of the railways

had made itself felt and most of the regular traffic to Rothesay already went by train and steamer, either via Greenock (Prince's Pier) or Wemyss Bay, while Largs and Millport were served from the latter and Arran from Ardrossan.

In short, the picture of Clyde steamer services at the turn of 1876/7 was that of a low-cost operation, still governed by practices which dated back to the beginning of steamboat services in these waters. But Victorian affluence was growing, and the time was ripe for something better.

New steamers of 1877

The year got off to a bad start with a period of sustained stormy weather in January, which had particular consequences for the Wemyss Bay fleet of Gillies & Campbell. On Saturday 13th the *Lady Gertrude* failed to stop on the approach to Toward Pier and ran aground. After some alarm, all the passengers were safely landed over the ship's stern on to the pier, but attempts to tow her off failed, and during the next week she went to

Passengers on board the *Elaine* c1880. The degree of overcrowding and the use of umbrellas for protection against smoke and smuts are clearly evident. *McLean Museum & Art Gallery*

pieces under the stress of further bad weather. Her machinery (but not the boiler) was salvaged.

By far the most important development was the formation of a new company to operate a luxury steamer for the service to Inveraray. Until then, passengers who looked for a premium service went by Hutcheson's *Iona* to Ardrishaig and thence by coach. The new service was therefore a direct attack on Hutcheson's position. The new company was the Glasgow & Inveraray Steamboat Co, and the driving force behind it was Malcolm T. Clark, Manager of the Lochgoil & Lochlong Steamboat Co. The Caledonian Railway was supportive, its Greenock agent, James Gilchrist, being one of the four shareholders. A large new ship was ordered from D. & W. Henderson of Glasgow, which was also responsible for the diagonal oscillating engines. Both Captain William Barr of the Lochgoil company and David Sutherland, who was to be responsible for catering on board, worked closely with the builders in matters of design. Completion of the ship was affected by labour troubles, in the form of a lockout of shipwrights which lasted from 1 May 1877 until the autumn, in one of the nastiest incidents of industrial history in the area, and she was finally launched in an incomplete state on 30 May, when she was christened *Lord of the Isles*. She was luxuriously furnished, perhaps the only drawback being that the settees in the saloon still faced inwards and any view over the stern was cut off by the ladies' cabin at its after end.

The *Lord of the Isles* took up service on the new route on 2 July, when the travelling public could see that a worthy rival to the Hutcheson ship was now on the Firth. The steamer left Greenock at 8.15am and returned from Inveraray at 2.15pm,

The *Lord of the Isles* at Rothesay Pier between 1885 and 1891. The Wemyss Bay steamer *Argyle* lies at the other end. *Ian Maclagan collection*

day excursionists having about an hour ashore there. Despite her incomplete state and some complaints about vibration, the *Lord of the Isles* was an instant success and gave a severe jolt to the complacency of Hutcheson's, which retaliated with the magnificent *Columba* in the following year. The credit for the former's success of her first season was due in equal measure to three men — her captain Robert Young, David Sutherland and Malcolm Clark.

Robert Young was clearly unusual among contemporary Clyde captains. His first command had been the Campbeltown steamer *Herald* of 1866. In the following year she was sold off the Firth, and Young moved on to command the new *Elaine*. Not only did he become recognised as a very competent skipper, but his ship was known as one of the best-managed steamers on the Clyde, and Young's approach to what would now be called 'customer relations' no doubt had much to do with this. At a time when Clyde skippers were not noted for their sartorial elegance, it was said that in the course of a working day he would change his clothes three times, and his habit of wearing kid gloves when on board earned him the nickname of Captain Kidd. It was not surprising that he should have been chosen to command the new tourist steamer, but unfortunately he remained with her only for one year and then retired from nautical service to become a music teacher. In the 1880s Donald Downie was given command and remained on the bridge for the rest of the vessel's Clyde career, then transferring to her successor. According to the *Oban Times* he was noted for his 'urbanity of manner and unremitting attention to the comfort of his passengers'.

Nor did Sutherland remain with the *Lord of the Isles* for much longer, since he moved to Oban in 1880 as lessee and manager of the new Great Western Hotel. However, a glance at the menu offered on board during his stewardship will show how far catering had developed from that offered on most river steamers. Breakfast was served on leaving Prince's Pier, Dunoon, and Wemyss Bay and, at a charge of 2s, there was a choice of salmon steaks or herring, in addition to the more usual fare. Lunch, at the same price, was served from 10.00 to noon and was clearly something of a snack meal, perhaps intended for servants, since its menu was restricted to soup, salmon or cold meats, cheese and oatcakes. What was

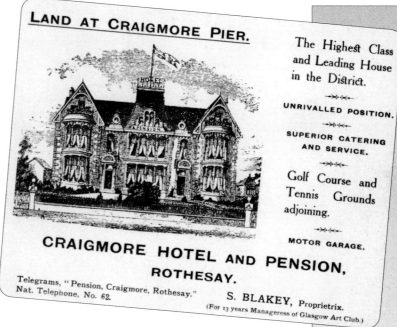

▲ An advertising card for the Craigmore Hotel.

termed dinner was served in two sittings, at 12.15 and 2pm, costing 3s. It offered soup, followed by a choice of salmon, roast beef, boiled mutton with caper sauce, roast lamb with mint sauce or cold cuts, all with green peas and other vegetables. Sweets or cheese and salad finished the meal. Tea could be had between 4pm and 6.30pm and was basically a choice of cold meats with the option of a boiled egg. But perhaps the main clue to the social standing of the passengers was contained in the smaller print at the foot of the menu, in which, among other sundries, malt liquors and cigars were offered. This was no ship for the pipe-smoking working classes, who would certainly have found it difficult to afford a day excursion, since the return fare from Glasgow via Greenock to Inveraray, Saloon and Second-class rail, was 6s 5d, and a day trip, with dinner, for a family of two adults and two children, would have absorbed almost all of a skilled worker's weekly wage. But the quality of catering and the choice of dishes set by Sutherland were to remain standard

for a century. On-board catering was also profitable — in 1934 the Caledonian Steam Packet Co (CSP) ships recorded a surplus of £4,026, almost all earned in the three summer months.

Malcolm Clark had been born on Loch Fyneside, at Strachur. He was the first manager in the business of running steamers to recognise the tremendous potential offered by combined tours by Clyde steamer, loch steamer, rail and coach. Day-cruise passengers were therefore catered for by no fewer than four circular tours in conjunction with sailings by the *Lord of the Isles*. The first was a circular tour by coach which was offered from Inveraray through Hell's Glen to Lochgoilhead, where passengers could join one of the Lochgoil steamers for the return to Greenock. In 1878, however, the company arranged a more ambitious round trip, which became known as the 'Famed Loch Eck day tour' and, in altered form,

continued to be offered as long as the Inveraray cruise remained in the timetable. A small 'gondola' steamer, the *Fairy Queen*, was built in the yard of another shareholder, T. B. Seath of Rutherglen, taken to pieces and re-launched, in pouring rain, on Loch Eck in February 1878. Coaches, with coachmen arrayed in scarlet uniforms, were bought to run between Dunoon or Kilmun and Inverchapel, at the south end of the loch, and Locheckhead, at its northern end, and Strachur, where a new pier was constructed. The *Oban Times* referred to these as 'finely finished and conspicuous conveyances', and they must have been a fine sight. The other tours involved a coach trip to Dalmally and return by the newly-opened Callander & Oban Railway and also a drive through Glen Croe to Loch Lomond, with a steamer run down to Balloch and train back to Glasgow. The later 'Circular tours by train, steamer and motor', which remained popular into the 1960s, were based directly on this venture.

Clark also pioneered the idea of inclusive short breaks, in conjunction with the Argyll Arms Hotel in Inveraray. Passengers could enjoy a round trip with one night's accommodation at the hotel for 20s or a Saturday to Monday break with full board on the Sunday for 30s.

The *Lord of the Isles*' contribution to coastal shipping development was not over when she was sold off the Firth after the 1890 season, a new ship, of the same name, having been ordered for 1891. She was acquired by the Victoria Steamboat Association for service on the Thames, and thus paved the way for the construction of ships such as the *Koh-i-Noor*. To these she also bequeathed her attractive red, white and black funnel colouring. She returned to her native river in 1903, being renamed *Lady of the Isles*, and went to the scrapyard in 1905.

The loss of the *Lady Gertrude* was turned to advantage by Gillies & Campbell in the acquisition of a fast steamer for the Rothesay service, which was growing in importance as a commuter route. The construction of the elegant terraces and villas such as Elysium Terrace (1875) and Royal Terrace (1877) had led to the building of a new pier at Craigmore, which was opened for traffic on 29 March 1877 by Gillies & Campbell's *Lancelot*. The prospectus for the Craigmore Pier Co Ltd stressed not only the saving of time which it would afford to local travellers but also 'its privacy … compared to the bustle of a large public quay'. There was also the Craigmore Hotel, 'patronised by the best class of tourists and visitors', according to the MacBrayne guide. A steady flow of First-class-season-ticket-holders and affluent tourists awaited whichever steamer could offer a fast service to the new pier as well as to Rothesay itself, and the Caledonian Railway and Gillies & Campbell were determined that much of this should come their way. Despite the advantage of location held by Wemyss Bay, the route was handicapped by the old and inconveniently sited terminus of Bridge Street in Glasgow, which compared badly with the Glasgow & South Western Railway's centrally-located St Enoch station, opened in 1876. The GSWR's 4.3pm evening express reached Prince's Pier in 47 minutes and

A Great Northern Railway poster for the Loch Eck Tour, showing one of the 'conspicuous conveyances' in full cry. *National Railway Museum / Science & Society Picture Library*

connected there with the speedy *Sultana*, commanded by the skilful and popular Captain James Williamson. Passengers could be in Rothesay by six o'clock.

The new steamer was named *Sheila* and ran trials on 18 May, when, according to newspaper reports, she attained a speed of 20mph. Under the command of Captain Duncan Bell she was placed in service on the morning and evening commuter runs to Rothesay, with a day trip to Lamlash in Arran in between, and soon proved that she was a match for the *Sultana*. A new express was put on from Bridge Street at 4.35pm, on which no heavy luggage was conveyed — a practice which later became general on coastal commuter trains — and passengers were in Rothesay at 5.55. Unfortunately her speed fell off after some years, and in 1882 she was sold to the North British Steam Packet Co.

The island of Arran was beginning to attract some holiday traffic, and the third steamer of 1877, a twin sister of the *Sheila*, was launched for another operator, Shearer Bros. Its ship was named *Glen Rosa* and, like her sister, was a flyer. However, the regular steamer on the run from upper Firth piers to Arran,

Keith's *Guinevere*, was already popular, and the excursion traffic to Arran did not call for high speed and was as yet inadequate to support two ships. Despite a price war, a good deal of racing and a spectacular — but fortunately not serious — collision between the rivals off Garroch Head, the Shearers withdrew and the *Glen Rosa* was sold in 1881.

The last new steamer of 1877 was also built for Gillies & Campbell and was launched as the *Adela* on 13 August, construction having been delayed by the shipyard lock-out. She had none of the glamour of the *Sheila* but was a plain vessel of moderate speed, of the type which has always been relied upon to maintain the year-round service on the Clyde. When Gillies & Campbell went out of business in 1890 she was sold to owners in Sussex. She ended her days plying in Corsican waters.

In their individual way, each of the new ships of 1877 — the luxury tourist steamer, the racy commuter flyer, the fast Arran excursion ship and the humble year-round plodder — exemplified the trends which were to operate on the Clyde for the next 100 years.

2. THE COMING OF THE RAILWAY STEAMERS

Prior to 1877 there had been unsuccessful attempts by local railway companies to operate steamers on their own account. Having burned its fingers with the first of these, the Caledonian Railway settled for a service provided by private operators via Custom House Quay at Greenock, 10 minutes' walk through insalubrious streets from its terminus at Cathcart Street. Its agent in the town, James Gilchrist, was a man of considerable presence and kept the steamer owners more or less under railway control. The Greenock & Wemyss Bay Railway, which was worked by the Caledonian, opened its line in 1865, but its over-ambitious attempt to run its own steamers was a failure, and in 1869 it arranged for Gillies & Campbell to provide a connecting service. Only the North British had been able to learn from its mistakes in 1866, when it briefly and extravagantly entered the Ardrishaig trade in competition with Hutcheson. In 1869 it re-opened its service from Helensburgh, but this time as a commuter run to the Holy Loch. The NBR had realised that wealthy commuters were a useful source of revenue, and the area around the entrance to Loch Long and the villages of the Holy Loch had become the location of some very desirable summer residences, often known as 'marine villas', for rich businessmen from Glasgow and Paisley. The developer of much of this area, an Irish mason named J. MacElroy, gave a lead in 1850 when he commissioned for himself, from the Glasgow architect Alexander 'Greek' Thomson, the Italianate villa of Craig Ailey at Kilcreggan. Not only the villas but also the local churches and other civic facilities reflect the wealth which was concentrated in the area. As the *Dandie Dinmont* had been built to take on the Hutcheson fleet, her facilities offered a standard of comfort far above that of other local steamers, and the new venture proved to be modestly successful and led to continuous operation of railway steamers on the Firth for exactly a century. The North British ships operating out of Silloth were from 1863 owned by the North British Steam Packet Co, which was simply a group of NB directors, and the Clyde steamers were entrusted to this organisation also. Helensburgh Pier would be enlarged in 1871.

C. S. P. Co. Ltd. (STMR. 4)
CLYDE RIVER STEAMER CLUB
CHARTER
16th. April 1966
Helensburgh, Gourock,
Dunoon OR Rothesay TO
TARBERT & ARDRISHAIG
WITH CRUISE. AND BACK.(I

On 23 December 1869 the Greenock & Ayrshire Railway opened its new station and pier at Greenock, originally referred to as 'Albert Harbour', later as 'Prince's Pier', and instituted a through rail/steamer service to Dunoon, the Holy Loch and Rothesay, Captain Alexander Williamson (Sr) and other private operators providing the steamers. The station was a substantial wooden building but was 114yd from the pier itself, and at some date between 1874 and 1880 a covered way was constructed to provide some shelter for passengers. The line was formally amalgamated with the Glasgow & South Western Railway in 1872. The confident forecast of the *Greenock Telegraph* of 7 January 1870 that the new line would see 'thousands of travellers … in the tourist season' proved to be correct, and slowly but very surely a marked loss of coast traffic to the Caledonian Railway ensued. By the early 1880s 80% of south-bank traffic went by the new route and at busy times there was acute congestion at Prince's Pier, with steamers having to lie two-abreast to embark passengers.

In 1872 the NBSP began a service to the Gareloch, where development had begun at an earlier date. Among early residents was Robert Napier, shipbuilder and engineer, who commissioned West Shandon House in 1852 to provide not only suitable living quarters for his family but also to house his collections of works of art, including some Rembrandts, and rare plants, obligingly brought back from Africa by David Livingstone. To provide a service to the loch, the railway company had built the pretty little steamer named after it, the *Gareloch*. The main disadvantages of this route were the distance between the pier and the railway station in Helensburgh — a fair 10-minute walk — and the inadequacy

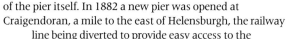

CALEDONIAN
Excursion Programme
AND **COAST** TIME TABLE

Via GOUROCK
WEMYSS BAY &
ARDROSSAN

SEASON
1908

of the pier itself. In 1882 a new pier was opened at Craigendoran, a mile to the east of Helensburgh, the railway line being diverted to provide easy access to the steamers, and over the years it acquired a loyal following among the travelling public. This loyalty was certainly increased by the adoption in 1883 of 'Scott' names for the steamers and an inspired new livery of cream saloons and red funnels with a white band separating the red from the black top — a livery which can still be seen, in slightly modified form, on the *Waverley*. Services were then extended to Rothesay.

On the north bank of the river, the Caledonian Railway was still smarting at the losses inflicted by the opening of the route via Prince's Pier but had to wait until 1884 before it could do anything about the situation. In that year it obtained powers to extend its Greenock line by almost three miles (half of this in tunnel), to a new terminus to be built on the shore of Gourock Bay. There was strong support from Malcolm Clark of the Inveraray company, who clearly felt that his passengers were not always treated at Prince's Pier with the attention they deserved, and from the owners of the *Ivanhoe*. Spoil from the tunnel excavations was used to reclaim land at Gourock, on which was constructed a new pier affording very easy same-level interchange between train and ship. The pier actually opened for traffic some time before the railway line was ready, in 1887. The whole enterprise cost £620,000.

The Caledonian originally planned that connections to and from its new pier should be provided by private operators, but due to the lack of enthusiasm shown by these it was decided in the autumn of 1888 that the company should apply for powers to run its own steamers, and it appointed Captain James Williamson of the *Ivanhoe* as Marine Superintendent, on a salary of £600 per annum. Unfortunately its Bill was rejected by Parliament in March 1889 — embarrassingly near the date set for the opening of the new route to the coast. The solution adopted was to set up the Caledonian Steam Packet Co Ltd, with a nominal capital of £64,000, to which were transferred the two

steamers already acquired and two which were nearing completion. The actual paid-up capital was only £70, being made up of seven £10 shares held by seven directors. Somehow — perhaps because of the wealth, power and position of its chairman, the Marquis of Breadalbane — the CR got away with this arrangement, and no-one ventured to ask how a company with a capital of £70 could manage to spend almost £100,000 on new ships and facilities. Services via Gourock began as planned on 1 June 1889, using new rakes of carriages. In the following year Captain Campbell withdrew his steamers from the services operating out of Wemyss Bay, and on 1 May CSP ships appeared there. In the same year an Ardrossan–Arran service was begun from the former's new Montgomerie Pier, in connection with the newly-opened Lanarkshire & Ayrshire Railway, which was worked by the CR.

While the new routes seemed to get off to a good start, carrying 405,187 passengers in the period up to February 1890, 905,176 in that calendar year and 1.137 million in 1891, matters were much less rosy financially. Only the Wemyss Bay steamers made a modest working profit, and almost all the other routes had to be heavily subsidised by the parent company. It was only the growth of total passenger numbers to around 4 million — a result of the increasing prosperity of Victorian Britain — that prevented the Clyde services' becoming a financial nightmare for all participating companies.

The immediate result of the new service was a complete haemorrhage of traffic from Prince's Pier. The number of passengers carried fell from 291,300 in 1888 to only 101,437 in 1890, and there was a particularly marked decline in the number travelling with the important tourist steamers. Worse still, Captain A. Williamson (Sr) had to be paid a subsidy of £1,500 to keep his steamers on the route at all.

It was natural that the GSWR would not (and, indeed, could not) stand aside to let its rival scoop all the coast traffic, and in 1891 it applied for powers to run its own steamers. The Act which resulted granted the powers but severely limited the sphere of operation, the west coast of Arran, Kintyre and Loch Fyne ports being barred to the company's ships, as was the River Clyde itself. It was also stipulated that the GSWR could run only services which connected with its trains, while

the CSP steamers could provide local services, such as that from Glasgow to Kilmun; it was probably for this reason that, when excursion services were begun from Ayr by the GSWR, through rail connections with these were always carefully advertised. Captain Alexander Williamson (Jr) became Marine Superintendent.

To complement the new fleet, Prince's Pier itself was completely rebuilt with four terminal platforms. Interchange was vastly improved, new stairways and ramps easing the flow of passengers, and luggage was catered for by several lifts. The whole was set off by buildings of a handsome Italianate style, designed by James Miller, and the new complex, which cost over £67,000, was formally opened on 25 May 1894. After the ceremonies, the invited guests enjoyed a cruise to Loch Striven on board the *Neptune*. As Prince's Pier was also an international terminal, being used for tenders serving transatlantic liners, customs and baggage halls were provided, and these remained in use until 1965. Arriving liner passengers used the east ramp. (The ramps would also prove useful during World War 2 for dealing with simultaneous heavy flows of embarking and disembarking troops.) For the boat trains, new rakes of bogie carriages were built, though unfortunately locomotives of adequate pulling-power for these did not arrive until some years later. However, despite this, the whole exercise regained for the GSWR much of the traffic it had lost.

The scene was thus set for several years of fierce competition, to the delight of commuters, enthusiasts and town councils in the resorts, but it was a heavy drain on the finances of the railway companies. Competition was especially severe between the Caledonian and the GSWR, but the NBSP was soon drawn into the fray and into spending on five new steamers — much more than it could properly afford. Even as early as 1894 there were suggestions for co-ordination of services, but it was not until 1909 that agreement was at last reached on this point, and from that year the CSP and GSWR fleets, despite frequent tensions, effectively became one unit.

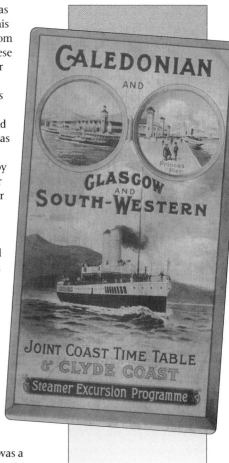

A view of the pier buildings at Craigendoran from a steamer in September 1964.
T. J. Edgington

▲ **Helensburgh**
The original North British terminal consisted of a single berth at the end of a fairly long jetty, constructed in 1816 and greatly improved in 1859. Despite its length, access at low water was always a problem for Helensburgh, and timetables carried a symbol denoting that steamers might not call at low tide. Regular services ceased for many years after the 1951 season, but in more recent times, thanks to calls by the *Waverley* and a year-round ferry service to Kilcreggan and Gourock, the pier has once again become a terminal.

Craigendoran
In 1882 a new pier was opened at Craigendoran, a mile to the east of Helensburgh, with a deviation of the railway line to provide easy access to the steamers. The new pier, built out into very shallow water, had accommodation for four vessels, though more could come alongside at certain times, and a curving bay platform allowed boat trains to wait clear of the main line. The station buildings were single-storey, of brick,

and Craigendoran had none of the architectural merit which would distinguish later terminal piers on the south bank, but it nevertheless provided easy same-level interchange facilities.

Custom House Quay, Greenock
From 1841 to 1869 this was the principal downriver terminal for Clyde steamers. After the opening of Prince's Pier, services declined, though a few calls continued until 1915. Today the wheel has turned full circle, and in summer the Quay sees regular use by the *Waverley*. The surrounding buildings have been cleaned, and the Quay is probably a more attractive terminal than at any previous time in its history.

Prince's Pier, Greenock
Opened in 1869, Prince's Pier permitted through rail/steamer services to Dunoon, the Holy Loch and Rothesay. In the 1890s it was completely rebuilt with improved interchange facilities and buildings in Italianate style, in which form it survived until demolition in 1969.

Gourock
There had been a stone quay at Gourock for many years when the Caledonian Railway purchased it in 1869, but another 20 years were to elapse before the CR could begin its new service from a new pier, 780ft in length, designed by architect James Miller (1860-1947). Although the buildings, in a Tudor style, were pleasant enough and the layout was practical, the pier somehow lacked a focus, and one of the first acts of the new CSP board was to order a clock tower for its western end.

Wemyss Bay
This is the Clyde terminal *par excellence*. The original railway pier was opened in 1865 and was a rather uninviting open structure, with an awkward staircase down from the platform, and the station was dark and gloomy. The pier was extended between 1899 and 1901, and in 1902/3 the station

was completely rebuilt by the Caledonian, which here surpassed even its own record for attractive stations. An inclined covered walkway linked the much-enlarged station with the steamer berths, and the exterior was given new buildings with a Queen Anne-style clock tower. James Miller was again the architect, but Donald Matheson, the CR's Engineer-in-Chief, also had much to do with the design, and, following his ideas, the station was not only handsome but practical, in the matter of dealing with large flows of passengers. Although the pier itself has been shortened and all shipping activity is now concentrated on the western side,

the entire structure has been magnificently restored and can still be enjoyed today.

Ardrossan
None of the terminal piers on the lower Firth showed any degree of architectural merit. Of Fairlie (1882) it may be said that no-one shed a tear when it was burned down immediately after closure in 1972. The two Ardrossan piers — Montgomerie Pier (CR, 1890) and Winton Pier (GSWR, 1892) — were not much better. Both have now been closed and replaced by a single uncovered platform.

The *Waverley* alongside the pier at Helensburgh on 16 April 1966, prior to working a charter cruise to Ardrishaig, to celebrate the centenary of the first North British sailing.
Author

By 1969 there was less traffic at Craigendoran, as shown by this view of the *Caledonia* (1934) and the *Maid of Argyll* at the pier.

The station at Prince's Pier, Greenock. BR Standard Class 4 tank No 80025 has just uncoupled from a Canadian Pacific 'Empress Voyager' boat train on 14 May 1964 and is preparing to run round. The train standing in Platform 2 is the dedicated rake of five ex-LMS corridor coaches plus BR luggage van which was set aside for these workings. The 612 headcode was used for the CP liner expresses, while those connecting with Cunard sailings carried 416. The last liner special ran on 30 November 1965. *Stuart Rankin*

A view from Platform 3/4 at Prince's Pier, looking towards the booking office. One of the ramps to the pier can be seen leading off to the left; the stairs down were located on either side of the booking office. *Stuart Rankin*

In 1881, when Gourock was still a tranquil little holiday resort, the *Elaine* of 1867 passes with a good crowd on board, bound for Rothesay. The coastguard look-out is on the extreme left; on the beach is a shooting range. *McLean Museum & Art Gallery*

Often to the inconvenience of passengers, the Clyde steamers shared Custom House Quay at Greenock with MacBrayne's ships and with cross-channel vessels. One of the former — probably the *Cavalier* of 1883 — is seen alongside. *Author's collection*

A charming postcard of Gourock Pier, apparently on a windy day, after the addition of the clock tower. The steamer leaving is not a CSP vessel but the *Edinburgh Castle* of the Loch Goil fleet. Her skipper, William Barr, was the last of the old-style Clyde captains and was famous for wearing a hard, brown felt hat when on duty and also for bringing his pet collie on board. He was a kindly, hospitable man, and visitors were made welcome on the bridge, where he would regale them with stories from his long life, such as that of when, as a boy about 1830, he had walked across the Clyde at Kelvinhaugh during a period of low water. He celebrated his golden jubilee as a master at the age of 85 in 1905 and retired at the end of that season. Inactivity clearly did not suit him, and he died soon afterwards. Although the card has been painted in a rather impressionist style, the enormous paddle boxes which graced this ship are very apparent. *Author's collection*

GOUROCK, The Pier.

▲ The pier at Wemyss Bay, seen from an approaching steamer in August 1966. The *Talisman* (1935), in her last season, lies at what was then known as the Millport berth, today used by the Rothesay car ferry.
T. J. Edgington

◄ The tradition of floral displays on the main concourse was maintained by British Railways, as seen here on the evening of 31 July 1967.
A. S. Clayton / OnLine Video Archives Ltd

The clock tower at Gourock disappeared in LMS days and by June 1953, when the *Jupiter* (1937) was recorded loading for Dunoon, the pier had resumed its original outline. *Author*

All the pre-Grouping railway companies built locomotives designed especially for the Clyde Coast traffic. One such class was Dugald Drummond's 'Coast Bogies' of 1887. No 82 of this class waits to leave Gourock on a Glasgow express. The engine was rebuilt in 1904 and withdrawn by the LMS in 1927. The class was successful on the Gourock road but less so when confronted by the gradients of the Wemyss Bay line. *Caledonian Railway Association*

From 1935 until the 1970s an attractive feature of the covered walkway at Wemyss Bay was the display in glass cases of paddle-box crests of former steamers. Here is shown that of the *Duchess of Hamilton* of 1890.
T. J. Edgington

Interior view of Ardrossan's Montgomerie Pier station on 22 June 1962, with Fairburn tank No 42196 on a railtour. *Harold D. Bowtell, Caledonian Railway Association*

4. SOME RAILWAY STEAMERS

Duchess of Hamilton (1890)

In August 1889 plans for a new steamer were drawn up, and the CSP board discussed these at its October meeting, the minutes of which refer to a new steamer for services from Ardrossan to Arran and Campbeltown. That meeting was adjourned to allow for discussion with the CR board; when it was resumed, all mention of services to Campbeltown had been dropped, and it was resolved to invite tenders for a steamer for the Arran service. The prices quoted varied widely, the dearest tender being that of A. & J. Inglis of Pointhouse at £37,000 and the cheapest that of Denny Bros at £24,000. The latter must have been cutting corners, since it was asked to submit an improved tender at the same price. This it duly did, and so was conceived one of the only two paddle steamers this firm built for Clyde service in the period under review. There were suggestions that the *Duchess of Hamilton* was actually built for service in Australia, but this has not been confirmed by records in either country; there may have been some confusion with the very fine paddle steamer *Hygeia*, which was also constructed on the Clyde in 1890, by Napier & Miller of Old Kilpatrick, for services at Melbourne, or perhaps the CSP allowed the rumour to circulate to hide its own activities!

Contemporaries waxed lyrical about the beauty of the new ship and Captain James Williamson referred to her as 'the finest and most successful craft in the Clyde passenger traffic'. The paddle boxes proudly carried the crest of the dukes of Hamilton and Brandon. But whatever her merits, the new steamer was an economic disaster area for the CSP. Initially she scooped the Arran traffic, carrying 82,300 passengers in 1890, but when the GSWR replied with the *Glen Sannox* of 1892, her carryings dropped to about 68,000 per annum. In 1893 she was in commission for 134 days, during which she carried 68,308 passengers. Working expenses, which included repairs but not depreciation, exceeded receipts by 1s 2d per mile, and, as she steamed 16,550 miles, she was subsidised by the CR to the tune of £960. As she had a crew of 42, this on many days gave a passenger:crew ratio of 3:1, which was excellent for the passengers but not for the finances of the CSP!

Her prestige was recognised in another sphere also. During the Clyde yachting 'fortnight' in July each year, one of the more palatial

The main saloon has been converted into a dining saloon in this view. Given the degree of floral decoration, this may well have been taken while she was acting as club steamer.
Ian Maclagan collection

steamers was chartered to act as club headquarters, becoming
both a floating office and grandstand. For many years the
chosen ship was the *Duchess of Hamilton*. While James
Williamson lamented the inconvenience of having one of
his best steamers thus removed from ordinary service, the
kudos (and probably the financial reward) was clearly too
great to refuse.

After 1906 the *Duchess of Hamilton,* re-boilered at a cost of
£2,350, was transferred to excursion work on the upper Firth
— a 'new and welcome feature', according to the CR
guidebook. On 6 June 1909 she took the first ever CSP Sunday
sailing, to Rothesay. Although there was still opposition to
'Sabbath-breaking', there were none of the rowdy scenes
which had marked previous attempts to run Sunday
steamers, and almost 400 passengers had an enjoyable day.
As the crew were paid time and a half, they probably enjoyed

themselves too. At this time a seaman was paid 27s per week
in summer.

The *Duchess of Hamilton* was lost while minesweeping in 1915.

Galatea

Built by Caird & Co of Greenock as the leading ship of the
CSP's new fleet in 1889, the *Galatea* was one of the Clyde's
disappointments. She was well furnished and made an
excellent subject for CSP posters, but her paddles were located
too far forward for satisfactory operation, and her powerful
machinery could not fully be utilised for fear of straining the
rather tender hull. From about 1901 there were constant
problems with her machinery and boilers, and in September
of that year the CSP Board resolved that firm offers of £10,000
should be sought for her. There were no takers. By the
following year, the price had dropped to £6,000, but still no

Gourock Pier

sale resulted. Finally, in June 1906, she was sold for £1,400, and the CSP was so anxious to be rid of her that it would in fact have accepted £1,100. To put this in perspective, it should be mentioned that in 1911 the CSP was able to sell the *Ivanhoe,* by then 31 years old, for £4,000. The *Galatea* went to Genoa and sailed there for a further seven years. Her memory is still commemorated in the name of a bar in Rothesay.

Caledonia

The first new steamer to be commissioned for the CSP, the *Caledonia* went on to become one of the most successful members of the fleet, albeit in a background role. She was built by John Reid & Co at Port Glasgow at a cost of £14,000, and, as J. Reid was a great-nephew of John Wood, builder of the *Comet* of 1812, the new steamer could claim a direct link with the Clyde's pioneer. She herself was also a pioneer in several respects. She was the first steamer on the Firth to use navy boilers working under forced draught and also the first to have docking telegraphs to allow her captain to communicate easily with crew members working the ropes as she came alongside a pier. These avoided the shouting of instructions, often accompanied by choice epithets, which, when in English (they were often in Gaelic) upset middle-class Glasgow and his wife. She was also the first in which the engine room was fully open to public view. Under-cover accommodation was provided for all passengers that she was licensed to carry.

At first the *Caledonia* was closely identified with the Gourock–Rothesay service, but after 1902 she gravitated to the Holy Loch service and remained on it for the rest of her career. She proved to be a good sea-boat and a most economical steamer. She was in commission all the year round, apart from overhaul periods and war service from 1917 to 1919. Her last run, in 1933, was celebrated with a dance on board at Kilmun.

It was a tribute to the reputation of the little ship that in 1902 and again in 1908 shipbrokers expressed great interest in purchasing her on behalf of other operators. The offer was refused on both occasions.

Marchioness of Lorne (1891)

Having been so successful with the summer Arran traffic in 1890, the CSP board then considered the question of the winter service. A proposed charter of the former Arran steamer *Brodick Castle,* then sailing in English waters, fell through, and in the event the route was left to Captain Buchanan for the winter of 1890/1. In modern parlance, the CSP could be accused of 'cherry picking'. However, it was determined to be in a better position in the following year and

briefly considered the idea of building a twin-screw steamer for this run. Tenders for this and a paddle steamer were received in September 1890. The idea of a screw steamer was dropped, but an order for the paddle steamer went ahead, to Russell & Co of Port Glasgow.

It was decided to name her *Marchioness of Lorne* after the Queen's daughter, Princess Louise. There was no need to write formally to HRH, as Lord Breadalbane undertook to have a word with her to seek her agreement. This was obviously forthcoming, and the new vessel was launched on 25 April 1891. On trial she did not reach her contract speed, and £100 was deducted from the payment to the builders, bringing her cost down below £16,000. In service she did not cover her working expenses, at least in her first few years, and she seems also to have been somewhat accident-prone. One of her captains was William Gordon, who, unusually among Clyde skippers, hailed from the east coast of Scotland. On the frequent occasions when his charge suffered the humiliation of being passed by older and smaller vessels, he was wont to philosophise "Ay, she's a smert boat and we'll no' be the first she has passed today".

With the co-ordination of services, in 1909 she was offered for £12,500 to a broker who had been enquiring about the possibility of buying one of the newer ships. He declined the bait, and the *Marchioness of Lorne* survived in the CSP fleet until requisitioned for minesweeping in 1917. She survived in a very bad state and was laid up in Bowling Harbour while her owners wrangled with the Admiralty over compensation. There was no point in reconditioning her, and the LMS was glad to sell the rusty hulk for scrap in the autumn of 1923, for £740.

Duchess of Rothesay

To the intense annoyance of the CSP, the GSWR in 1894 began to run a steamer to Arran via the Kyles of Bute, thus offering direct competition to the now ageing *Ivanhoe*. The company took legal action against the competition (a battle which it ultimately lost), but, having considered building two new steamers, it also took the practical step of ordering one fine new ship from J. & G. Thomson of Clydebank, at a cost of £19,900. She was named *Duchess of Rothesay* (the Scottish title of the Princess of Wales, who did not, in fact, make any use of

it), and for the first time the CSP got it right with a large ship. Faster than her contract speed, she soon became a firm favourite and remained so until the end of her Clyde service in 1939. The CSP clearly regarded this vessel, along with the *Galatea* and the *Duchess of Hamilton*, as a front-rank member of the fleet; whereas the meat ordered for consumption in other ships cost 8½d per pound, that for these three ships cost 9d! The Royal connection was maintained at intervals throughout her career, in 1897, 1907, 1914 and 1920, and she carried more members of the Royal Family than did any other Clyde steamer. For such trips she was specially decorated, but the CSP, though flattered, did not allow its head to be turned; for the visit of 1914, the cost of the decorations was not to exceed £25.

Having served with distinction in both world wars, the *Duchess of Rothesay* was broken up in the Netherlands in 1945.

▲ Here the *Duchess of Rothesay* has exchanged her beautiful livery for naval grey, as a minesweeper, and members of her crew are seen investigating an object which looks suspiciously like a mine.
McLean Museum & Art Gallery

The *Caledonia* at Prince's Pier after the pooling agreement of 1908 had come into force.
Author's collection

PRINCE'S PIER, GREENOCK.

The Caledonian Railway excelled in its publicity material, including postcards of the steamers. This is the official *Marchioness of Lorne* card.
Author's collection

Duchess of Argyll

It was in the autumn of 1904 that the CSP first thought of acquiring a turbine steamer, but plans submitted by John Brown & Co were declined, and it was not until the autumn of the following year that an offer from Denny's to build such a steamer for £30,000 was accepted. The new ship was handsome and speedy, at over 21 knots, and CR publicity described her as a 'floating palace'. Her arrival coincided with the introduction of new 'trains de luxe' — compartment versions of the Grampian 12-wheel corridor stock — on coast services. It was resolved by the CSP Board that she would be kept solely on the Arran run. Sadly, she had scarcely time to make her mark there before the pooling agreement of 1908

deprived her of a chance to relegate the *Glen Sannox* to second place, and she spent the next few years on a variety of services, including Larne–Stranraer relief sailings. The CR guide of 1914 nevertheless proclaimed that 'The Turbines are becoming more popular every year — the travelling public enthusiastically appreciates the improved method of propulsion. The entire absence of vibration now makes pleasure sailing an enjoyable as well as an invigorating and healthful pastime.' However, there could be sad moments too, and the last prewar CSP Board minute records a fatal accident to a passenger on board the *Duchess of Argyll* on 28 July 1914, exact details not being given.

She really found her niche, after a distinguished war record,

▲ The *Duchess of Argyll* comes alongside Dunoon Pier in 1951. Most of the after deck has been cleared to leave room for cars and cargo. *W. J. Wyse, courtesy Light Rail Transit Association (London Area)*

A postcard view of the
Duchess of Argyll in 1912.
Additional lifeboats have
hastily been lashed to the
promenade deck, following
the loss of *Titanic*.
Author's collection

on the service to Arran via the Kyles, which she made her own from 1919 to 1935, and then on the Campbeltown and Inveraray sailings until 1939. She remained on the Firth during World War 2 and thereafter was used on ferry sailings, for which she was not really suited. Her lack of astern power was a drawback, and she was cruelly nicknamed 'the Slow Boat to Rothesay', the song 'Slow Boat to China' being one of the hits of 1949. Sold to the Admiralty in 1952, she served as a floating laboratory until scrapped in 1970.

Viceroy

To start its new services, the GSWR acquired a very mixed bag of six steamers, of which one of the better ones was the *Viceroy*, built in 1875 for Captain Alexander Williamson Snr but lengthened and fitted with deck saloons in 1891. She remained in service with the railway until 1905 and was sold for service in North Wales, as the *Rhos Colwyn*.

Glen Sannox (1892)

For the Arran service the GSWR was determined to have a ship which would surpass the *Duchess of Hamilton*, and in October 1891 it placed an order with J. & G. Thomson of Clydebank for a large steamer for this route. When the *Glen Sannox* appeared in May 1892 it was clear that all concerned had created a ship which would be one of the Clyde's best in every respect — comfort, looks and speed (19.7 knots) — and she completely fulfilled her owners' expectations. She was the most expensive Clyde steamer yet built, her cost of £30,000 plus £229 for 'extras' not being exceeded until the construction of her replacement in 1925. She was the first Clyde steamer to be plated up to the bow, and in her grey-and-white livery, with red funnels, she looked magnificent. Her speed allowed an acceleration of the service, and passengers on the 8.5 departure from Brodick were able to reach Glasgow St Enoch at 9.25. True, there were not nearly

A photograph, taken at a pier in the Holy Loch, showing the *Viceroy*'s enormous paddle wheels and (on the forward sponson) the galley chimney, painted to match the funnel.
T. J. Edgington collection

Making a good deal of smoke, the *Glen Sannox* calls at Lamlash. The forward fore-saloon windows are boarded over against possible storm damage. Well over a dozen herring skiffs can be seen at the stone pier.
Robert Grieves collection

enough of these commuters to fill a ship of her size, let alone the Caledonian steamer, but she regained for her owners all of the traffic that they had lost in 1890 and more, and her initial cost and running expenses were considered well worthwhile.

Much has been made of the *Glen Sannox*'s appetite for coal, and this has been held to explain her rejection by the Admiralty for trooping service in 1915, after she had made a couple of trips from Southampton to Le Havre. In fact, compared to her contemporaries, she was not notably extravagant, and, given that the Admiralty was happy to employ coal-guzzlers like *La Marguerite*, the rejection may have been more to do with the fragile nature of her sponsons, which had been damaged on passage; she had a history of problems in that area, going back to damage sustained in a summer storm on 16 June 1897. In any case, she was a very useful member of the home fleet for wartime traffic and passed to LMS control in 1923. That company did consider re-boilering her in 1924, but when it was discovered that substantial additional repairs would be necessary, at a total cost of over £40,000, it seemed better to scrap her and build a turbine replacement.

Neptune and Mercury (1892)

To operate its new services the GSWR ordered two steamers from Napier, Shanks & Bell of Yoker, at a cost of over £19,000 each. They were designed to outclass their CSP rivals, and both were capable of over 18 knots in service. They were also more substantially built. There were some teething troubles, with the engine framing and paddle shafts, but both ships soon settled down to give excellent service and won back much traffic for their owners. The *Mercury* principally served on the Rothesay/ Kyles of Bute service, while her sister, after spending some time at Ayr as a cruise ship, was used for longer excursions from Greenock. The *Neptune,* renamed *Nepaulin,* was lost while minesweeping on 20 April 1917, but the *Mercury* survived the loss of first her stern and then her bow, to return to service in 1920. But the war seems to have taken its toll, and in the 1920s she was no longer in her prime, judging by the number of complaints made about her timekeeping. She was sold for scrapping in 1933.

Minerva and Glen Rosa (1893)

By the beginning of 1893 it was clear that the GSWR's venture was successful, and it was decided to order further new tonnage. However, it was thought prudent to order only one ship at first and a second only if the proposed sale of the *Scotia* went through for £6,000. In the event it proved difficult to dispose of her; in January 1893 an initial enquirer backed off when he learned of her coal consumption; then in July a sale to one M Thionnet of Paris likewise fell through. She was finally sold by auction in September, for £5,300, and went off to the Bristol Channel. In the meantime it had been decided to order two new vessels anyway, but the delay explains why the two were not exact sisters. The offer of the builders, J. & G. Thomson of Clydebank, to build two ships for rather less than twice the cost of a single ship may also have influenced the decision.

The *Minerva* and the *Glen Rosa* were tough little ships, well suited to the winter Arran service, and proved, at 17.5 knots, to be faster than their contract speed of 16 knots. Both were eagerly snapped up by the Admiralty in 1915 and 1917 respectively. The *Minerva* was sent to the Mediterranean and was captured by the Turks, to whom she was sold at the end

of the war. She lasted until 1927 or 1929. Her sister, rebuilt under the LMS regime, was withdrawn in 1938.

Jupiter (1896)

The competition of the years 1890-5 certainly had the effect of stimulating traffic, to the extent where it was sometimes difficult to cope with numbers. On Easter Monday 1895, for example, there were some alarming scenes at Dunoon Pier in the evening, when passengers overwhelmed the crews of both CSP and GSWR ships and several sailed with numbers acknowledged to be above their official complement. It was against this background that the GSWR decided that it was necessary to build another new ship to deal with coast traffic, and J. & G. Thomson was approached to build an 18-knot steamer for £22,000-23,000. The result was the *Jupiter*, which also exceeded her contract speed and proved to be another greyhound; usually employed on the service to Arran via the Kyles of Bute, she totally outclassed the *Ivanhoe* in every respect. In LMS days she was relegated to ferry services and was withdrawn in 1935.

Vulcan

The first part of this steamer's history is complicated. In 1897 Captain John Williamson had ordered a steamer for his up-river traffic but had sold her before completion to the Hastings & St Leonards Steam Boat Co, which named her *Britannia*; as such she was reasonably successful but no match for the steamers of P. & A. Campbell.

An impressive view of the *Glen Rosa* at speed. The use of a canvas dodger around the deck rails was unusual on the Clyde, though common elsewhere.
McLean Museum & Art Gallery

The *Jupiter* was relegated to ferry services in LMS days and is here seen coming alongside Hunter's Quay.
T. J. Edgington collection

In 1904 she was sold back to Captain Williamson, who immediately offered her to the GSWR for £6,100. As this was a bargain price for a fairly new and very economical ship, the railway company jumped at the chance and in return also gave the elderly *Marquis of Bute* to Captain Williamson.

The *Vulcan* was placed on the Fairlie–Millport–Kilchattan Bay service and in due course became involved in what became known as the Battle of Millport Pier. In 1906 Millport Town Council gave the railway companies notice that annual pier dues would be increased from £150 to £512 per annum. The Council had bought the pier in 1905 and had just spent £9,000 on extending and improving it, but the town's ratepayers were growing restive. The competitive railway companies were quick to unite against a common foe and protested vigorously but to no avail, and announced that they would suspend services after Saturday 30 June. The *Vulcan* made the last GSWR calls that evening, uplifted the company's gangways and sailed off to the strains of 'Will ye no' come back again?'. The matter was ultimately resolved by the intervention of David Lloyd George, then President of the Board of Trade, and the steamers returned to the town on the following Thursday, initially at the old rates.

With the pooling agreement of 1908, the *Vulcan* became redundant and was sold back to Captain Williamson for £9,000 — the only occasion on which a company made a cash profit on selling a ship.

Lucy Ashton

It is strange to recollect that this little ship, which went on to become one of the Firth's legends, might well have had only a very short career on the services from Craigendoran, for which she was built in 1888. As early as November 1899, the board of the North British Steam Packet Co minuted that a firm offer for her would receive consideration, and by May 1900 negotiations for her sale were in hand. She was in the meantime laid up and apparently needed a fair amount of work. As the prospective purchaser wanted her to be ready for service with a Class 3 certificate by July — a condition which it would be impossible to fulfil — the deal was not completed, and by November it was decided to spend £3,000 on a new boiler and other repairs by Inglis. She re-entered service in 1901 but on 16 December broke down rather publicly when coming alongside Prince's Pier and had to be withdrawn again. This time she received a new compound engine, after some dithering on the part of the Steam Packet Co, which, concerned at the likely cost, also obtained a tender for a single diagonal engine. Fitting a new engine of this type would have been a very retrograde step, but, when it is realised that the company had an overdraft of £120,000 with the British Linen Bank, the concern of board members is understandable. In the event, when it became apparent that a single engine would cost £5,300, it was decided to go ahead with compound machinery, and a rejuvenated *Lucy Ashton* was handed back to her owners on 28 May 1902. Unfortunately the new boiler of 1901 was incompatible with the new machinery, and another had to be fitted, but the 1901 boiler went into the *Lady Rowena*. The total cost of all the work on the two ships was £7,886 12s 8d, of which £5,000 was paid on account by the NBSP, leaving the NBR to pay the balance after the Steam Packet Co was wound up in the autumn of 1902.

◄ A postcard view
showing the *Vulcan*
off Fairlie.
Author's collection

By 1914 thoughts of replacing her had again surfaced and a new ship, the *Fair Maid,* was built by Inglis, but she was immediately commandeered for minesweeping and was lost on active service. The *Lucy Ashton* soldiered on until 1939, when the axe was again suspended over her, but a total machinery failure on the *Talisman* and then the outbreak of war saved her again, and she went on to perform the most heroic service of her career, single-handedly maintaining the LNER services until June 1946, with only a few days off in 1944. British Railways tactlessly repainted her funnel yellow in 1948, and she made her last run for BR in February 1949. Even then she cheated the scrappers and, fitted with jet engines, spent two very noisy years carrying out tests on hull resistance for the British Shipbuilding Research Association. The end finally came in the autumn of 1951.

Lady Rowena

This steamer was built for the Arrochar service in 1891, the NBSP having taken it over from the Loch Long Co. She was luxuriously furnished, and the *Glasgow Herald* enthused over the damask curtains and velvet upholstery in the saloon.

Unusually for the time, the dining saloon was placed on the main deck forward, there being no accommodation on the lower deck aft, its traditional location; diners could thus enjoy a view of the scenery with their meals, instead of having nothing better to contemplate than water surging over the portholes. The *Lady Rowena* seemed to be a pretty little 'butterfly' boat, intended for summer operation in sheltered waters. Like many butterflies, she proved in the event to be quite tough and came to know waters which were anything but sheltered. Having been sold by the NBR in 1903, she had a spell in the Gulf of Naples before returning to work out of Brighton and then returning to the Clyde in 1911, where we will meet her again.

Redgauntlet

Although built for the Rothesay service, the *Redgauntlet* was used from 1898 on cruises from Craigendoran. The very large plate-glass windows in her saloons made her ideal for sightseeing, and her amenities were improved by the fitting of a new dining saloon in the lower deck aft. In 1899 her master, Captain Gillies, was transferred to the new *Waverley* and

The *Lady Rowena*
off Gourock.
McLean Museum & Art Gallery

The *Lady Rowena*
off Gourock.
McLean Museum & Art Gallery

The *Redgauntlet*
in early days on the Clyde.
Author's collection

replaced by Captain MacPhail. Her regular Wednesday cruise was round Arran, and on 16 August about 120 passengers were enjoying or enduring a trip down the west coast of that island in somewhat cold and blustery weather. Just after 2pm, she rounded Drumadoon Point and then, with a horrible grating noise, struck a ledge known as the Iron Rock, off Sliddery. Those who were below rushed on deck as water poured into the dining saloon, and, relates the *Ardrossan & Saltcoats Herald*, 'the greatest excitement and alarm prevailed', with the women and children becoming hysterical. (Presumably the male passengers simply kept a stiff upper lip!) Perhaps Captain MacPhail had not as yet learned all the tricks of his new command, or perhaps he had not made sufficient allowance for the strong sea running on his starboard quarter, but he made up for any error by promptly going to the wheel himself and beaching the steamer. No-one was injured in what came close to being one of the Clyde's few disasters, although the women and children were 'severely shaken, all more or less suffering from the severe shock to their

nervous systems'. The passengers were taken ashore through 'fearful breakers' in the ship's lifeboats, with some assistance from local people, who also put them up for the night. As they left Lagg the next morning in brakes for Whiting Bay, many looked back down on the *Redgauntlet* and, seeing the waves breaking over her stern, expected her to become a total wreck. The *Lucy Ashton* took them back to their various destinations, not reaching Craigendoran until the afternoon.

Fortunately the *Redgauntlet* did not break up and on 25 August was salvaged by the Clyde Salvage Co, at a cost of £1,500. Repairs cost £5,737 14s 9d, to which expense had to be added damages from passengers settled for £336 13s (this being 55% of what was originally claimed, the lawyers having been told to keep the amount down), the cost of hiring a lawyer to represent the owners at the Board of Trade inquiry and the costs for the inquiry itself. The NBR steamers were not insured, and, all in all, the adventure cost the company almost half the price of a new ship. It is no wonder that Captain MacPhail was downgraded to mate for a while. As the Steam Packet Co did not have the resources to meet the expenses it had to go cap-in-hand to the NBR itself for payment, and the incident probably had much to do with the decision taken in 1902 to remove the Clyde steamers from the NBSPC and place them under direct railway control.

The *Redgauntlet* herself was none the worse for her accident and sailed on until 1909, when she was transferred to the Forth, where she proved popular. After wartime minesweeping, she was sold to French owners and was used at Oran until 1934.

Waverley (1899)

In 1898 the NBSP Board decided to seek tenders for a new steamer designed for long-distance cruising work. Only two yards tendered, suggesting that the specification was over-exacting, and the contract went to A. & J. Inglis for £24,200. The company's traditional canny approach seems to have been abandoned, and the result was a thoroughly modern paddle steamer, equipped with compound diagonal engines and extensive saloon accommodation. But there is some evidence that there was a cash-flow problem in funding such a large outlay; the payment to the builders due in May 1899 was delayed for a month, and the last instalment was not paid

until 28 September — almost three months after the *Waverley* had entered service. Whatever the financial problems, the NBSP had given the Clyde one of its best and most loved steamers, and she sailed with great success until laid up in 1939. She was reactivated on the outbreak of war and on 29 May 1940 went down at Dunkirk, with some loss of life. However, her master, Captain Cameron, survived to bring her successor into service in June 1947 and, later, see this ship pass into preservation.

◄ During her military service in World War 1 the *Waverley*'s promenade deck was extended to the bow, and this was retained, with some effect on her speed, on her return to civilian duties. In this condition she is shown backing out of Lochgoilhead Pier, with the stern of Williamson-Buchanan's *Queen-Empress* in the foreground. *Robert Grieves collection*

5. SOME SMALLER PIERS

Before the advent of the motor vehicle, road travel in the Clyde area, for both passengers and goods, was slow, expensive and uncomfortable. Every community therefore wanted its own passenger pier and very often also a cargo jetty, and the Clyde saw the construction of a plethora of piers serving individual localities, these often being within sight of each other.

The average Clyde pier was a simple wooden jetty, extending as far from the shore as necessary to allow steamers to come alongside at all states of the tide. Typically there would be a stone building at the pier head, incorporating a small office and the piermaster's house, while on the pier itself there would be a white-painted wooden shelter. In the heyday of separate services, each of the three railway companies wished to serve the same pier at more or less the same time, and peak-hour congestion and racing became a problem. To counter this, a signalling apparatus was developed and fitted to most piers from 1890. This took the form of black discs in a white box which sat atop the structure on the pier and was worked from it.

Kirn

Kirn lies about a mile to the east of Dunoon and developed as an affluent suburb of the latter. There was a pier by 1845, but sustained development of the area began in the 1890s, and, after completion of the promenade in 1893, the pier was completely rebuilt two years later. Alone among the smaller piers, Kirn showed some architectural merit in its pier-head buildings. These consisted of an attractive cottage-style building and an entrance surmounted by a clock tower and two red brick drum towers in a vaguely baronial style. The architect was H. E. Clifford.

Traffic declined after World War 2 and an unsuccessful attempt to close the pier was made by British Railways in 1951. Thereafter, it received, in summer, only three calls in each direction on weekdays (Monday-Friday), with an extra one on Saturdays. The morning up commuter steamer was still timed to the minute — she left at 7.33 — in the last example of this kind of timetabling on the Firth. Final closure came in December 1963, the last ship to call being the *Cowal*.

In this view dating from 1949, the *Duchess of Argyll* is seen calling while a puffer discharges cargo at the stone quay. Kirn seemed to offer all the ingredients for a successful holiday — in the foreground, boats are offered for hire, a bicycle is parked against the boat hirer's shed and, just beyond it, children can be seen enjoying themselves in the paddling pool. *Robert Grieves collection*

Hunter's Quay

This pier provides the only example on the Clyde coast of a village being named after its pier! In 1828 an enterprising entrepreneur, Robert Hunter, seeing the possibilities of commuter traffic offered by the steamers, bought Hafton House (1816) and estate and began feuing[1] plots of land for the construction of 'marine villas'. Soon the area had a good quota of well-to-do inhabitants, many of whom travelled daily to and from Greenock or Glasgow, and the entire coastline round to Dunoon was built up. A hotel was opened in 1857, and the stone quay constructed by Hunter when he acquired the estate was replaced in 1858 by a more

1. A Scottish legal term for letting out land for development under strict conditions.

commodious wooden pier. Closure came in September 1964, but in 1969 the pier was bought by a company acting for Western Ferries, and on 3 June 1973 the latter opened its car-ferry service to/from MacKinlay's Point on the opposite shore. A slip was constructed to the north of the pier, which today serves as a breakwater. With a minimum half-hourly frequency, much increased at peak periods, Hunter's Quay is now busier than it ever was.

The area around the pier developed as a holiday resort in a slightly different way from the traditional Clyde manner. The hotel was burned to the ground in 1887, and in 1888/9 a replacement, in the style of a Tudor country house and having 41 bedrooms, was built by the architect T. L. Watson for his brother G. L. Watson, designer of many of the great yachts, such as the Prince of Wales' *Britannia* and Sir Thomas Lipton's

▲ Western Ferries' *Sound of Shuna* at the pier at Hunter's Quay, when acting as relief vessel. This ferry had inaugurated the service on 3 June 1973. *Author*

Captain MacLean's *Marquis of Bute* calls at Hunter's Quay *en route* to Rothesay from Greenock and Glasgow *c*1880.
McLean Museum & Art Gallery

In 1949 the *Marchioness of Lorne* (1935), on the Holy Loch service, pauses at Hunter's Quay to set down some passengers.
Robert Grieves collection

The LNER's *Kenilworth* leaves Hunter's Quay bound for Craigendoran in the 1930s. *Author's collection*

Shamrock II . This hotel incorporated office accommodation for what was then the Royal Northern (and later became the Royal Clyde) Yacht Club. Especially during the 'Clyde fortnight' in July, Hunter's Quay became a mecca for the wealthy and famous. Although the great yachts have gone, the Royal Marine Hotel, modernised but scarcely altered, is still very much in business.

Innellan

Apart from the ruins of the 16th-century Knockamillie Castle (which have since vanished) there was nothing in this area five miles west of Dunoon until feuing began in 1843. Thereafter many fine villas were constructed, mostly in a Gothic style, and these attracted wealthy residents, such as the Coats family (of thread-making fame) from Paisley. To cater for these, a pier was constructed in 1850/1, and the location of what had now become Innellan allowed it to receive calls from the Wemyss Bay steamers after 1865, in addition to those sailing from Greenock and, later, Gourock.

Although a large hotel (the Royal) was built in the Scottish Baronial style, the village always remained secluded. The pier was extended in 1900, as it was unusable at low water by some of the new steamers. To finance this work, pier dues were introduced — a move which aroused considerable opposition. Passenger numbers dwindled after 1945, and the last call in normal service was made by the *Waverley* on 30 September 1972. The pier was reopened from March to October 1974 for workers' services to/from the oil platform construction yard at Ardyne.

Toward

No-one who has sailed on the Firth of Clyde can have missed Toward lighthouse. After a good deal of agitation by the people of Bute, this was constructed in 1812, and a small village grew up around it. Possibly to stimulate further development, a pier was opened in 1863, but, despite its convenient location, the anticipated development did not happen. There was no building of large villas, and even a

The *Cowal* leaving the pier at Innellan after uplifting a crowd of Ardyne workmen in May 1974. *Author* ▲

A view of Toward village from the pier, with little sign of activity! *Author's collection* ▶

Toward,
The Lighthouse from Pier.

tenement block looks as though it has not been finished. In fact there was latterly so little traffic that only the Caledonian steamers called on service runs. It was, however, a popular destination for evening cruises, often by Williamson's *Kylemore* from Rothesay and Largs, and her passengers would go ashore and dance on the beach to the light of flaring torches. The pier closed as early as October 1922.

Craigmore

As already mentioned, this pier was constructed in 1877 to serve Rothesay's affluent suburb. Unusually for the Clyde, the landing stage was of iron, which by 1888 had corroded badly. Unfortunately the 'privacy' mentioned in the prospectus of the company which built it meant that there would be insufficient passengers to make it pay; in 1889 the Craigmore Pier Co had to be wound up and the New Craigmore Pier Co was formed to rebuild the pier head (in wood) and operate it.

This company was financially more successful, and thereafter the pier provided a useful service until closed in October 1939. It was then demolished.

Tighnabruaich

Along with Kilcreggan, this is the only small pier still in use on the Clyde, although its future has recently been in question. Unusually the waiting area and the signalling apparatus were located halfway down the pier, rather than at its end.

Unfortunately there is no record of the date of the construction of the pier, but it was probably first erected in the 1850s, when feuing of the district began. It was completely rebuilt in the winter of 1884/5. There was some summer commuter traffic, but the village is located just too far from the railheads for this to have developed on any large scale, and it has long since ceased. The *Waverley* is now the only large ship to use the pier.

A group of passengers prepare to board the *Jeanie Deans* at Tighnabruaich in July 1960. *Author*

Although there was little in the way of 'amusements' at Craigmore, some children are enjoying donkey rides in this pre-1914 view of the GSWR's *Mercury* calling *en route* to the Kyles of Bute.
McLean Museum & Art Gallery

An idyllic scene on 30 May 1955. The *Queen Mary II* rests at the pier at Tighnabruaich after coming down from Glasgow on the 11am sailing while a group of holidaymakers relax by the shore and two ladies, complete with hats, prepare to enjoy a picnic.
T. J. Edgington

Keppel

This pier was erected in 1888, to act as a relief to the Old Pier in Millport, and was formally inaugurated by the *Adela* on 18 August. Despite her being received with 'much enthusiasm', the company which had built the pier was in chronic financial difficulties and regularly petitioned the two main railway companies for assistance — a plea to which they just as regularly turned a deaf ear. It was finally taken over by Millport Town Council in 1905. Regular use by excursion steamers from 1927 brought more traffic, but after 1960 passenger numbers declined, and the pier closed in January 1972, the last vessel to call being the *Cowal*, which seems to have developed a penchant for closing piers.

Clynder

At one time this Gareloch village boasted two piers within 500yd of each other — the official Clynder Pier and Barreman Pier. The latter had been constructed by a local landowner to encourage feuing of the area and, because of its superior facilities, gradually gained most of the traffic, Clynder Pier closing in 1892. In due course Barreman Pier was renamed Clynder, but it too closed, in the autumn of 1942.

Kilchattan Bay

This pier at the south end of Bute was opened in 1880 to serve the local community and for almost all of its existence was served by the Millport steamers. It also had a fair amount of cargo business, and its only excursion traffic was that of circular tours in Bute, passengers proceeding to Rothesay, by horse brake until 1914, thereafter by bus. However, between 1932 and 1938 the LNER's *Jeanie Deans* called on some of her cruises to Arran, Ayr and round Ailsa Craig. The pier closed in 1955.

◀ The *Jeanie Deans* alongside at Kilchattan Bay, sometime between 1932 and 1935.
Ian Maclagan collection

The *Duchess of Montrose* alongside
Keppel Pier in the late 1930s.
Author's collection

Children and some pier staff
pose for the camera at Keppel
*c*1900. *Author's collection* ▶

The *Lucy Ashton* calls at
Clynder's Barreman Pier
*c*1904. *Robert Grieves
collection*

THE FUNNY SIDE OF THINGS

The various incidents which often accompanied steamer travel were a good source of inspiration for producers of comic postcards.

SCENE : The dining-saloon of a steamer on the Clyde.

Voice from above : "Come up, Jock, come up! Here's the Kyles of Bute !"

Jock : "Deil tak' the Kyles o' Bute! D'ye think I'm gaun tae spoil ma holidays wi' scenery !"

The alleged meanness of the Scot!
Author's collection

"WHIT WEY IS'T A M NO SEEK, MAW ?"

"JIST, MA MANNIE, BECAUSE YE'RE GAUN DOON THE WATTER BY THE TURBINE, AN' NO BY THAE AULD PAIDLES."

'Knocking copy' for Turbine Steamers Ltd. It is not known who actually produced these cards, but the company could not have been displeased to have the superiority of its vessels thus advertised. Although 'Maw' looks rather elderly, the wee boy bears a fair resemblance to 'Wee MacGreegor' of the J. J. Bell stories, in which the steamers figure prominently. The steamer is identified as the *Queen Alexandra*, but the stanchions supporting the upper deck would suggest that she is actually the *King Edward*.
Author's collection

The frenzied efforts of those who arrived at the last minute were always a great source of amusement to those already safely on board. The ship is the *Lord of the Isles* (1891), with the *Minerva* beyond.
Author's collection

6. A VERY USEFUL BOAT

In Campbell's colours, the *Madge Wildfire* lies at the Broomielaw in 1886. The other steamers are the *Athole* (ahead) and the *Benmore* (astern).
McLean Museum & Art Gallery

There was nothing at all outstanding about the paddle steamer built in 1886 by S. McKnight & Co of Ayr for the Glasgow–Kilmun service of Captain Bob Campbell. The *Madge Wildfire* was just an ordinary little ship, with a plain but comfortable saloon for cabin passengers and a very basic single diagonal engine, totally lacking the glamour of ships such as the *Columba*. Yet in the end she would last far longer and work much harder than the MacBrayne veteran ever did.

In December 1888 the *Madge Wildfire* and her consort the *Meg Merrilees* were bought by the Caledonian Railway and registered in the names of two of its directors, passing upon its formation to the Steam Packet Co. The CSP thought highly of the little ship and invested in a new compound engine for her in 1891. She later gained a fore saloon to give some shelter to steerage passengers, and her bridge was moved to a position forward of the funnel. She stayed with the CSP until 1911, when she was sold to Captain A. W. Cameron for a very satisfactory £3,500. Captain Cameron was a retired deep-sea skipper who had served with the Wilson Line of Hull, and for 1912 the *Madge Wildfire* was given Wilson's attractive colours of dark green hull and red funnel with a black top. She was also fitted with a dining saloon. However, in March 1913 she was sold to Buchanan Steamers Ltd and renamed *Isle of Skye*. After three years of war service she reopened passenger sailings from Glasgow in the spring of 1919, and many must have been glad to see her back. In 1927 she was sold for service on the Forth and until 1939, as the *Fair Maid,* had a busy career as excursion ship, tender and occasional ferry relief. She came back to her native Firth in 1939 as a tender but also had a spell on passenger service out of Craigendoran, to relieve the hard-pressed *Lucy Ashton*. The rather demanding schedule was eased to suit her plodding gait, although a contemporary noted that this concession was probably unnecessary. For one day she also revisited her old haunts of the Holy Loch.

The *Madge Wildfire* won no races in her long career, no wealthy tourists ever trod her decks, yet she worked hard throughout her life and brought pleasure to thousands on both sides of Scotland. As she went off to the scrapyard at Troon in December 1945, there was the satisfaction of a job well done.

A postcard of
1913/4 showing the
Isle of Skye in her
Buchanan livery.
Author's collection

A sunset view of the
Madge Wildfire off Gourock
later in her time with the CSP.
Author's collection

The *Madge Wildfire* displays
the new colour scheme of
Captain Cameron as she
approaches Dunoon in 1912.
Author's collection

7. STEAMERS OF THE 1920s AND '30s

In Caledonian MacBrayne colours, the *King George V* revisits the haunts of her youth at Inveraray in 1974.
Dr Alastair C. Harper

The railway Grouping of 1923 made very little practical difference to the Clyde steamers, since the CR and GSWR fleets had been worked virtually as one unit since the war, and the only change made by the LNER at Craigendoran was the introduction of a new house flag. There were enough steamers to work all services, and for the time being there was little need of new tonnage.

King George V

The ship which made all earlier turbines obsolete at a stroke was the *King George V*, built by Denny Bros for Turbine Steamers Ltd in 1926 though not entering service until late in that season. 'The large, airy dining saloon … The cosy tea lounge and smoke room and ladies' cabin … all these and many more features bespeak the solicitude of the Management for their patrons' enjoyment.' So ran the publicity for the new ship, and it went on to explain, in layman's terms, her novel machinery, with its high-pressure turbines and water-tube boilers. In fact the machinery proved to be something of a liability, since the ship had to be re-boilered twice, in 1929 and 1935, and there were also two serious accidents on board, one involving the death of an engineer, quite apart from several breakdowns in service. Nonetheless, passengers loved the new facilities and in particular the fine dining saloon on the main deck aft, with its large windows.

The 'KGV', as she was popularly known, really found her niche when she was sold to David MacBrayne in 1935 and became the Iona cruise steamer in the following year.

However, she was still seen on the Clyde from time to time and in her last years was especially popular for charters, one of which took her to Bangor in Ireland, reviving a Burns Laird excursion of prewar years. There was great regret when she was withdrawn in 1974, and, sadly, proposed preservation schemes came to nought.

Duchess of Montrose (1930)

Naturally the CSP was alarmed at the impact of the new turbine, but it had some difficulty in persuading its LMS masters that a new steamer should be built, since at that moment it was not proposed to retire any existing members of the fleet, and a new vessel would have to be funded from capital account. But finally the CSP won the day, and the result was the *Duchess of Montrose*, a ship of a standard not hitherto seen on the Firth. Her cost — £76,800 — was also unprecedented and would not be exceeded until after 1945. As she was laid out for First-class passengers only, facilities did not have to be duplicated, and she had an air of spaciousness and luxury which soon earned her a loyal following. It also gave her a very easy life, since she could not be used on ferry runs on summer Saturdays. Her first years were not totally trouble-free — she rather embarrassingly broke down on her maiden voyage, and until 1934 there was a persistent problem with soot and grit falling on to the after deck, the remedy for which in the end cost the CSP an additional £680. But despite this she soon became a most popular steamer.

Her programme, from 1930 to 1939, was of cruises from Gourock to Ayr, 'Round of the Lochs', 'Around Arran' and 'Ailsa Craig & Inveraray'. Prior to 1936 she had sailed to Stranraer rather than the last of these. In 1939 the return fare

More often associated with the Inveraray service, the *King George V* is seen at Campbeltown in 1935, her last year of service with Turbine Steamers Ltd. *Author's collection*

In as-built condition, the *Duchess of Montrose* clears Rothesay Bay on one of her long-distance cruises in the lower Firth. Craigmore Pier can be seen behind her stern. *Ian Maclagan collection*

By July 1960 the *Duchess of Montrose* had regained her former elegance after war service. Here the setting sun picks out the gleaming paintwork as she is seen from the *Waverley* off Toward. *Author*

A colour poster featuring the *Mercury* and the *Caledonia*. The artist, Norman Wilkinson, clearly took pains to show the new concealed paddle boxes — only the wash from the wheels amidships indicates that the *Caledonia* was a paddle steamer. The *Mercury*, depicted somewhat inaccurately, is in the background. *National Railway Museum / Science & Society Picture Library*

The last full year of peace, 1938, was also that of the Empire Exhibition in Glasgow and marked the peak of inter-war Clyde services. Despite atrocious weather, many visitors came to Scotland and good loads were carried. This timetable carries the Exhibition logo.

In BR colours, the *Jeanie Deans* is seen coming alongside Craigendoran in 1951.
W. J. Wyse, courtesy LRTA (London Area)

This view, taken at Greenwich Pier in 1967, shows the LNER funnel colours by then restored to the *Jeanie Deans*.
Author

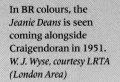

from Glasgow, by Third-class rail, was 7s 5d. Lunch would have cost 3s 6d and high tea 3s or 2s 6d, not leaving a lot of change from a weekly wage of perhaps £4. She was not a ship for the masses! *En route*, passengers would have enjoyed listening to music from the ship's orchestra — no mere band on this vessel — and could relax with a drink in the bar designed in the fashion of an Olde English country pub.

All this came to an abrupt end in September 1939, when she became the Wemyss Bay–Rothesay ferry steamer. For six years her saloons would be crammed with service personnel and the immaculate teak decks churned and scarred by the iron wheels of luggage barrows. She continued to be used as a ferry until 1948 and seemed to take some time to get over her wartime experiences. Conversion to oil fuel in 1956 brought back her old sparkle and increased speed, and she remained popular on long-distance sailings until withdrawn in September 1964.

Jeanie Deans (1931)

This was the LNER's response to the *Duchess of Montrose,* but, unlike the CSP vessel, the new paddler was laid out in the traditional manner, as a two-class ship. From 1932 to 1938 the *Jeanie Deans* was employed on long-distance cruises and no doubt gained some revenue from those who could not afford the fares on the CSP ship. After distinguished war service she was substantially rebuilt and became associated in particular with the new cruise around Bute introduced by British Railways. After withdrawal in 1964 she spent two rather unhappy years (1966/7) on the Thames before being scrapped in 1968.

Mercury and Caledonia (1934)

In 1934 the LMS introduced two new paddle steamers whose design caused a good deal of comment from those used to more traditional outlines. Concealed paddle boxes, high bridges and a streamlined outline all suggested a complete re-think of paddle-steamer design. Sir H. Arthur Rose, Chairman of the LMS Steam Vessels Sub-committee, was enthusiastic about the new ships and persuaded the company to arrange a special press cruise, using both ships, on Tuesday 8 May, in what proved to be rather blustery weather.

There were criticisms from traditionalists about what they considered the too-modern appearance of the new ships, and there were also some mechanical problems in the early years. But passengers appreciated the covered deck shelters and the excellent dining facilities, and the *Mercury* and the *Caledonia* soon settled down to be valued members of the fleet.

The *Mercury* was lost while minesweeping, but the *Caledonia* returned safely after the war and enjoyed a long career, sailing latterly from Craigendoran. In 1970 she was sold to become a restaurant ship on the Thames and was equally successful in that role until, sadly, so badly damaged by fire in 1980, she had to be scrapped, although her engines have been preserved.

8. THE TWO MAIN PIERS

The focal points of Clyde services have always been the two main resort piers of Dunoon and Rothesay. Both are large structures, and even today can accommodate two ships simultaneously. In its heyday, Rothesay could take seven and an overflow pier, the Albert Pier, could handle an additional vessel. But whereas Dunoon was almost entirely intended for use by passenger steamers, with only a very limited cargo capacity at the eastern end, Rothesay Pier was — and still is — only one part of a working harbour.

Probably for this reason, spectators were not welcome at Rothesay, there being nowhere for them to sit while viewing the activity, unless they perched on a bollard, from which they were liable to be summarily removed when the next steamer came in. Dunoon, on the other hand, especially from the 1930s, encouraged them with the provision of a tea room, music through loudspeakers and, in 1937, an observation gallery, for which a small charge was made in prewar years.

Dunoon had a small jetty from 1835, and in 1867 this was replaced by a longer structure, which was lengthened in 1881 and is seen here in 1895. The steamer alongside is the *Jeanie Deans* of 1884, as fitted with a deck saloon.
McLean Museum & Art Gallery

The present pier at Dunoon, seen from the upper deck of the *Waverley* in the early 1970s, when the observation deck still drew a large number of spectators. *Dr Alastair C. Harper*

The last passengers hurry aboard the *Waverley* at Berth 1 in June 1971 past the *Glen Sannox* which has just drawn in from Wemyss Bay at Berth 2. *Author*

Rivalry! Amid much churning of paddles, the *Columba* and the *Lord of the Isles* (1891) leave Rothesay simultaneously on a summer morning in the early 1900s. *Author's collection*

In 1895 Dunoon Pier was acquired by the Burgh Council from the Hafton Estate, and plans were immediately put in hand to enlarge it to a two-berth configuration. Not only was it enlarged but new buildings, in a Tudor style, were erected, and the pier-head buildings were also completely rebuilt. The whole new complex was formally opened in June 1898, and this Edwardian postcard shows it as a promenade of Edwardian elegance. A CSP steamer awaits departure. *Author's collection*

Rothesay Pier was often crowded with holidaymakers and normally the only sadness was that of end of the holidays. However, at 5.40 on the morning of 18 August 1914, the pier was crowded on a much sadder occasion — the departure of the first troops to the western front, aboard the *Duchess of Fife*. The *Duchess of Montrose* awaits her first normal sailing of the day at Berth 1.
Ian Maclagan collection

HALF DAY EXCURSION   HALF DAY EXCURSION
Afternoon Cruise from
Afternoon Cruise   *Afternoon Cruise*
Rothesay Pier   Rothesay Pier
ROTHESAY PIER
(H) 3/3   FARE   3/3 (H)
For condit'ns see over   For condit'ns see over
1287   1287

9. ALL THE WAY

The success of the new railway steamers led to a relative decline in the services from Glasgow to the coast. But completion of the Clyde sewage-purification scheme in 1904 and increasing prosperity of the Edwardian years encouraged a revival of interest in sailing 'all the way', though now almost always as a day excursion. The years immediately before 1914 saw two new ships built for these services and two new operators entering the market using second-hand tonnage. After 1919 they were the preserve of the newly merged Williamson-Buchanan fleet, apart from the early-morning departure of the MacBrayne and Campbeltown mail steamers. Williamson-Buchanan came under LMS control in 1936. Services continued with two steamers until 1952 and thereafter were worked by a single ship, normally the *Queen Mary II* of 1933.

Isle of Arran

This steamer was built for Buchanan Steamers Ltd by Seath of Rutherglen in 1892 and, with saloons fore and aft, marked a distinct advance in comfort for up-river passengers. Although not fast, she was a comfortable and well-liked ship. Following war service as a minesweeper she was rebuilt with the bridge forward of the funnel and continued to sail from Glasgow until Easter Monday 1933. She was then sold to the General Steam Navigation Co in London and was broken up in 1936.

Sultana

In 1897 Captain John Williamson bought back, for £750, his brother's old command, the *Sultana,* and placed her on the Glasgow–Rothesay service. No longer the flyer she once was, she was still a popular ship, and her acquisition allowed

◄ The Broomielaw. From the days of the *Comet* and her contemporaries, this was the traditional departure point for river steamers. This view taken *c*1902 shows Buchanan's *Isle of Bute* and, astern of her, the *Isle of Arran*. In the background, work is progressing on the enlargement of Central station. *Author's collection*

STEAMERS
SAIL DAILY
from
BRIDGE WHARF,
GLASGOW,
at 10 and 11 a.m.,
for
DUNOON,
ROTHESAY, and
KYLES OF BUTE.

For particulars see
Glasgow Newspapers.

P.S. ISLE OF ARRAN, OFF ROTHESAY

▲ A Buchanan publicity card showing the *Isle of Arran* in original condition at Rothesay. *Author's collection*

▲ There is scarcely a square inch of deck space left on board as the *Isle of Arran*, listing heavily to starboard, sweeps into Dunoon in the early 1920s. She was then employed on the 9.30 departure from Glasgow for Dunoon, Rothesay and a cruise round Cumbrae, at a fare of 4s 6d. Tickets inclusive of lunch and plain or high tea were also available. *T. J. Edgington collection*

◄ A deck view of the *Isle of Arran*. The passengers are well wrapped-up and do not seem to be enjoying the sail! The wooden awning was intended to double as a giant life raft but, perhaps fortunately, was not put to the test! *Author's collection*

The *Sultana* during her brief service with Captain John Williamson.
McLean Museum & Art Gallery

Williamson to place his new *Strathmore* on the Campbeltown run, in preparation for the arrival of the turbine steamers a few years later. The older ship was sold in 1899 to the Lochfyne & Glasgow Steam Packet Co and in 1900 to Spanish owners, for whom she sailed until 1907.

Lord of the Isles (1891)
After a valiant attempt to keep her owners' Inveraray service going in the teeth of turbine opposition, this steamer was in 1912 sold to that opposition and placed on a cruise round Bute from Glasgow. During World War 1 she continued to provide excursions to Lochgoilhead. Wisely, Turbine Steamers Ltd did not alter the distinctive funnel colouring, and the *Lord of the Isles* thus retained her attractive paint scheme, along with polished copper stem pipes, until broken up in 1928.

Lady Rowena
Usually when a steamer left the Clyde, she left it for good, but this ex-North British vessel was an exception to the rule. After sailing out of Naples and on the South Coast of England, she came back to Glasgow in 1911, when she was purchased by Captain A. W. Cameron, to join his *Madge Wildfire* on sailings to Dunoon, Rothesay and the Kyles of Bute. Captain Cameron seems to have aimed at the upper end of the Glasgow day-tripper market, since his fares were slightly higher than Buchanan's; in 1914 the cost of a day cruise including 'dinner' (lunch and tea) was 5s, as against 4s 6d.

NEW EXCURSION ROUTE

GLASGOW to DUNOON, ROTHESAY, KYLES OF BUTE and ROUND THE ISLAND OF BUTE

By the Magnificent Steamer

"LORD OF THE ISLES"

From GLASGOW, Broomielaw, Daily (Sundays excepted) at 10-30 a.m.

Calling at Govan 10-40 a.m., Renfrew 11-0, Gourock 12-25 p.m., Dunoon 1-0, Craigmore 1-30 Rothesay 1-50, Port-Bannatyne 2-0, Tighnabruaich 2-40, Kames 2-45 p.m., thence on a

Cruise Round the ISLAND OF BUTE

Returning from Rothesay 5-5 p.m., Dunoon 5-45

Arrives Gourock 6-5 p.m., Renfrew 7-30, Govan 7-50, Broomielaw about 8-5 p.m.

Passengers returning from KYLES may travel from TIGHNABRUAICH per "QUEEN ALEXANDRA" at 4.25 p.m. for GOUROCK and GREENOCK (Princes Pier).

RETURN FARES—	Saloon	F.-Sal.		Saloon	F.-Sal.
			Kyles Piers,	5/-	4/-
Glasgow to Dunoon,	3/6	2/6	Round Bute,	5/6	4/-
" Rothesay,	4/-	3/-			

WHOLE DAY'S SAIL (Saloon) with DINNER and PLAIN TEA, 10/-

AFTERNOON CRUISE FROM THE COAST

Leaving Gourock at 12-25, Dunoon 1-0, Craigmore 1-30, Rothesay 1-50, Port-Bannatyne 2-0, Tighnabruaich 2-40, and Kames 2-45

Round the ISLAND OF BUTE

RETURN EXCURSION FARES—	Kyles of Bute		Round the Island of Bute	
	Saloon	F.-Sal.	Saloon	F.-Sal.
From Gourock,	3/9	3/-	3/9	3/-
" Dunoon,				
" Craigmore, Rothesay	3/-	2/3	2/6	2/-
or Port-Bannatyne	1/6	1/-	2/-	1/6

DAY'S SAIL from GOUROCK with DINNER and PLAIN TEA, 8/6

NOTE.—Alterations may take place in the times advertised in this Programme, and Passengers are respectfully requested to consult Time Bills and Notices issued by the respective Companies. Connections are not guaranteed. TURBINE STEAMERS, LIMITED, and JOHN WILLIAMSON & CO. give notice that they will not be responsible for the loss of, or injury to Passengers, or their Luggage, arising from negligence or any other cause; nor for loss or delay through Steamers deviating from the usual route and calling at other ports, nor for Steamers not sailing as advertised.

JOHN WILLIAMSON & CO., 99 Great Clyde Street, GLASGOW, C.I.

◄ A handbill for the *Lord of the Isles*, post-1918.

▲ The *Lord of the Isles* leaving Glasgow on a cruise in the 1920s. *Author's collection*

Queen Mary

Despite the economic depression of the early 1930s, the up-river sailings were flourishing, and in 1933 Williamson-Buchanan commissioned one of the finest pleasure steamers of all time. Built by Denny Bros of Dumbarton at a cost of £61,805 16s 9d, she offered to those wanting to sail from Glasgow accommodation of the standard which had been set by the CSP's *Duchess of Montrose*. Unlike the latter she continued to offer two classes of travel, and, unusually, her First-class accommodation was forward and her upper deck extended almost to the stern. She was also of greater beam than any other contemporary Clyde steamer and was in all a most comfortable ship. Between 1935 and 1976 the numeral was added to her name to allow the Cunarder use of her original name. In 1957 a thorough modernisation and conversion to oil fuel saw her twin funnels replaced by one large funnel which, if anything, made her even more majestic. She sailed until 1977 — the last turbine pleasure steamer to operate anywhere — and, after being laid up for some time, was sold for use as a static restaurant ship on the Thames, where she remains. Her twin funnels have been restored.

The *Queen Mary II* heads away from Dunoon for Govan and Glasgow in July 1952. *Author*

The *Lady Rowena* paddling up the Kyles towards the Narrows, still retaining an awning over the after deck from her time in Italy. At this date — 1912/13 — she wore Cameron's attractive Wilson Line colours of green hull and red funnel with black top. *Author's collection*

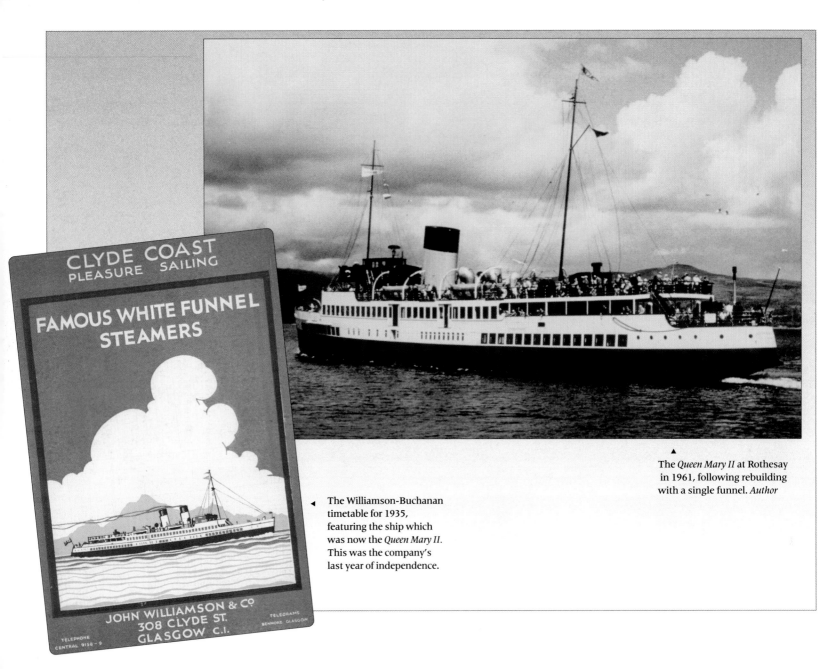

CLYDE COAST
PLEASURE SAILING

FAMOUS WHITE FUNNEL
STEAMERS

JOHN WILLIAMSON & CO
308 CLYDE ST.
GLASGOW C.I.

TELEPHONE
CENTRAL 9158-9

TELEGRAMS
BENMORE, GLASGOW

▲

The *Queen Mary II* at Rothesay
in 1961, following rebuilding
with a single funnel. *Author*

◄ The Williamson-Buchanan
timetable for 1935,
featuring the ship which
was now the *Queen Mary II*.
This was the company's
last year of independence.

Charters

In addition to scheduled services, much 'all the way' business was derived from private charters, and until the 1960s it was not unusual to see three or four large steamers sailing from Glasgow on a single day in May and June of each year. Charter rates were relatively low, and such cruises were popular for works outings.

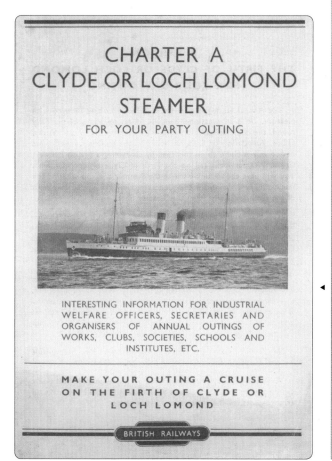

CHARTER A
CLYDE OR LOCH LOMOND
STEAMER

FOR YOUR PARTY OUTING

INTERESTING INFORMATION FOR INDUSTRIAL WELFARE OFFICERS, SECRETARIES AND ORGANISERS OF ANNUAL OUTINGS OF WORKS, CLUBS, SOCIETIES, SCHOOLS AND INSTITUTES, ETC.

MAKE YOUR OUTING A CRUISE ON THE FIRTH OF CLYDE OR LOCH LOMOND

BRITISH RAILWAYS

◄ A brochure of 1955, featuring the *Duchess of Montrose.*

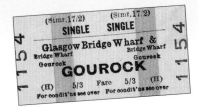

▲
In 1969 — the last year of sailings from Bridge Wharf — the *Duchess of Hamilton*, dressed overall, awaits a works party at Bridge Wharf while Kingston Bridge takes shape in the background. Unusually, she has not turned on her way upriver; turbine steamers normally turned at the entrance to Queen's Dock and arrived in Glasgow stern first.
Tom Hart

10. ARRAN PIERS AND FERRIES

"Ferry Left" Pirnmill.

Anderson's Select Series. Photo by I. C. E.

The development of Arran as a holiday area followed rather different lines from either the other Firth resorts or the West Highland towns. It did not cater for the industrial masses or for the very wealthy; instead, it became the paradise for the middle classes from Glasgow and further afield; in 1892 future Prime Minister H. H. Asquith brought his family to holiday at Lamlash and, sadly, while there, his first wife died. There was therefore no need for large piers, and ferry boats lasted longer in Arran than anywhere else on the Firth.

Pirnmill, on the west coast, retained its ferry until 1935, and a local stationer published a series of attractive postcards of it. Cycling was always a favourite pastime in Arran, and this card illustrates the difficulties of landing cycles by ferry in a rather choppy sea. *Robert Grieves collection*

Whiting Bay did not acquire its pier until 1899. In this 1913 view it plays host to the *Duchess of Argyll* (on the left) and the *Waverley* (right), the latter being on a charter. At the stone jetty the sailing boat *Champion* attracts the interest of holiday children. *McLean Museum & Art Gallery*

64

The route taken to Arran by the *Ivanhoe* was via the Kyles of Bute and her first landfall on the island was at Corrie, also served by a ferry which lasted until 1939. Interested spectators watch from the rocks as the ferry boat tenders her. *McLean Museum & Art Gallery*

Steamers did not call at Arran piers on a Sunday until 1959, and even then there was only an evening call at Whiting Bay to uplift returning weekenders. But the outbreak of war in 1914 led to a call of an unusual nature on a Sunday: there was a great demand for horses, and the War Office bought 80 from Arran owners, giving a good price. On Sunday 9 August the *Duchess of Argyll* made a special call at Brodick to transport the animals to Rothesay. Many people came down to the pier to watch, and one old man was heard to say: 'This is not like the Sabbaths we have been accustomed to in Arran!' *Isle of Arran Heritage Museum*

The first Brodick Pier in the 1880s. The steamer alongside is the *Ivanhoe*, in the colours of her original owners, the (*sic*) Frith of Clyde Steam Packet Co, by which she was run on temperance lines. *Isle of Arran Heritage Museum*

11. MACBRAYNE STEAMERS ON THE FIRTH

It is difficult to know what to say about the *Columba* — the 'world-famous floating palace' of MacBrayne's 1905 guidebook — but one factor which set her apart from all the other steamers on the Firth was the ratio of crew to passengers. The *Columba* had a crew of no fewer than 74 to administer to the passengers' needs. As her Class 5 certificate allowed her to carry 2,116 passengers, this gave a ratio of almost one crew member to every 30 passengers, even when she was most crowded. Compared to other steamers such as the *Madge Wildfire* (16 crew for 983 passengers, or 1:61.5) this allowed a high standard of personal service, but perhaps no more than passengers of the social standing she carried would expect. In 1913 even the august Central Hotel in Glasgow

('There is no more popular establishment among travellers of the better class', as the CR guide charmingly put it) was willing to provide a special early breakfast at 7am to those travelling on by train to connect with her at Gourock. It also allowed the company to enforce a strict regime on its passengers, concerning in particular the use of the saloon, in which a new arrangement of seating bays replaced the traditional longitudinal settees. The breakfast/dining saloon on the lower deck was furnished with a series of separate tables, and meals were served at any time. Passengers who had travelled overnight from England could enjoy a salt-water bath before being groomed in the 'shampooing and hairdressing establishment'.

The holidaymakers at Dunoon appear to be showing very little interest in the *Columba* as she sweeps majestically into the pier on her homeward run to Gourock, Greenock and Glasgow, at some date between 1903 and 1912. The rival attractions of motor-launch trips around the Gantocks (advertised on the board on the right) and an ice-cream seller's barrow at the water's edge have gained the upper hand!
McLean Museum & Art Gallery

In 1910 the Cabin day-return fare from Glasgow to Ardrishaig was 6s, or 10s 6d with lunch and tea. A comparable trip by one of the railway steamers, such as that from Gourock to Round Arran and Ailsa Craig by the *Duchess of Hamilton*, cost 5s by Third-class rail and Cabin, while a trip from Glasgow to Lochgoilhead aboard the old *Edinburgh Castle* cost only 2s return Cabin. A coach drive to Glendaruel from Colintraive was offered for 3s 6d, but generally the *Columba* catered for long-distance passengers rather than those on short day trips. Servants travelling Cabin had to pay full Cabin fare. The charge for a dog from Glasgow to Ardrishaig was 2s, but there was a separate tariff for sporting dogs.

Of course, like the travellers, the *Columba* herself was pampered. She was in service for (at most) four months of every year and, apart from the odd summer storm, did not have to contend with bad weather. In 1931 an anonymous author penned some lines as from the newly-withdrawn *Glencoe* to other members of the MacBrayne fleet. That to the *Columba* was honest to the point of sarcasm: 'I've faced the Minch and Jura Sound when you were snug in Bowling!'

For the crew, conditions were not so good. The schedule was demanding — in 1908 she was allowed only 13 minutes from Gourock to Dunoon — and punctuality was of the essence. Until electric light was installed in 1929 the engine room was particularly dark, and the stokers, charged with shovelling

18-20 tons of coal into her boilers daily, must have been glad when Glasgow was reached in the evening. In 1919 they, along with their colleagues on the *Lord of the Isles,* went on strike for an increase in their wages. They got most of what they requested. Such an incident would have been inconceivable pre-1914 — times were indeed a-changing!

Although the *Columba* was to last until 1935, the apogee of her career probably came on 31 August 1912, during the celebrations to mark the centenary of the sailing of Henry Bell's *Comet.* In preference to all other ships, such as the sleek new turbine *Queen Alexandra,* the *Columba* was chosen to convey the official party — including Mr T. MacKinnon Wood,

In 1910 A. & J. Inglis of Pointhouse, Glasgow, built the last 'paddler' for the MacBrayne fleet. Named *Mountaineer*, she had the unusual feature of solid boarding in place of the normal open rails around her promenade deck. Intended to increase the comfort of her passengers, this in fact made her fragile and difficult to handle in a strong wind, and ordinary rails later replaced it. In this view, off Shandon in the Gareloch, she appears to have a grey hull; during the latter part of World War 1 she was chartered to the North British Railway, and the photograph probably dates from this time. She was broken up in 1938.
McLean Museum & Art Gallery

MacBrayne's second and much less well-known Clyde service was the mail run from Greenock to Lochgoilhead, which the company inherited from the Lochgoilhead & Inveraray Co in 1912. In 1913 the old *Edinburgh Castle* was withdrawn and replaced by a small motor launch, fitted with a paraffin engine. She had been bought by MacBrayne in 1908 and from 1913 until October 1946 remained on the Loch Goil service. She was then replaced by a bus connection from Arrochar and was sold for service from Shoreham, Sussex. She is seen here backing out of Lochgoilhead.
Robert Grieves collection   COMET (III)

In October 1935 MacBrayne acquired from Turbine Steamers Ltd the steamers *Queen Alexandra* and *King George V*. The former was a direct replacement for the *Columba* and in the winter of 1935/6 was given a very extensive rebuilding, during which she was fitted with a third funnel, in a very obvious attempt to emulate the new Cunarder *Queen Mary*. The upper deck was extended aft, and under this extension was fitted a new smokeroom, designated the 'Clachan Bar'. These alterations turned what had always been a pretty ship into a most imposing one, and, in a different way, she was just as majestic as her predecessor. In 1937 she became the first Clyde steamer to be converted permanently for oil fuel. She served Ardrishaig from 1936 until 1939 and again from 1947 until withdrawal in September 1958; in this view she is seen sweeping away from Tighnabruaich.
T. J. Edgington collection

▲ The *Lochfyne* crossing Rothesay Bay on 8 April 1961. *Author*

◄ MacBrayne cargo services to the Hebrides were all worked to/from Glasgow, and the various cargo ships were a familiar sight on the Firth. Here the *Lochbroom* of 1948 is seen 'dropping the pilot' off Gourock on a July evening in 1967. In attendance is the Clyde Pilotage Authority's *Gantock*, based at Gourock Pier and normally moored alongside the west side. *Author*

The normal relief vessel for the *Lochfyne* was the *Loch Nevis* of 1934, seen entering Rothesay on the return journey from Ardrishaig in May 1959. *Author*

The *King George V* did not directly replace the *Iona* but did assume the relief duties on the Clyde which the latter had sometimes carried out. She is seen here departing Rothesay for Ardrishaig on 27 September 1952. *Author*

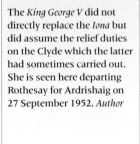

Chief Secretary for Scotland — downriver, leaving the Broomielaw at mid-day and returning at 6pm. *En route* there were two sittings for lunch, and the distinguished party was entertained by the orchestra of Mr W. H. Cole, whose repertoire included 'On the Rolling Sea' by Manaus, selections from Léhar and Sullivan and a 'Scotch' selection, entitled 'Carnegie', which Mr Cole himself had composed. Downriver, Admiral Sir John Jellicoe was in attendance on HMS *Hercules*, and yachts of the Royal Clyde and Royal Northern yacht clubs were present.

In 1931, as part of the reconstruction programme put in place by MacBrayne's new owners, the LMS Railway and Coast Lines Ltd, a revolutionary new ship was built for the company by Denny Bros of Dumbarton. The *Lochfyne* was the first diesel-electric ship to operate in British waters. Despite the associated noise and vibration, the new machinery proved its worth, and the ship was both economical and a good sea boat. She was used on the Ardrishaig run in winter from 1931 and also served it in summer during World War 2 and again from 1959 to 1969. She was then used for some years as an accommodation ship, and there were attempts at preservation, as a restaurant ship. Apathy and bureaucratic obstruction won the day, however, and sadly another pioneer went to the scrapyard, in 1974.

12. WEE BOATS AND BIG SHIPS

Passenger traffic on the Clyde was catered for not only by the steamers but by an assortment of smaller craft, some of which became as well known and loved as their bigger sisters.

To provide visitors to the 1938 Empire Exhibition with a chance to see the shipyards, the CSP commissioned from Denny Bros two small motor vessels to run trips downriver from Bridge Wharf to John Brown's yard at Clydebank. These were named *Ashton* and *Leven*. After war service as tenders at Gourock, they were briefly used on a Gourock–Dunoon ferry service before being transferred to run between Largs and Millport.

In 1965 the *Ashton* was sold to Mr R. Ritchie of Gourock for local ferry services and in 1968 was renamed *Gourockian*. Both ships were ultimately sold off the Clyde and are still afloat at the time of writing. The *Ashton* is based on the Humber as the *Wyre Lady* and was most recently in the news in June 2002, when she provided early-morning television cruises to allow football fans to watch the World Cup matches and enjoy a drink on board at the same time. The *Leven* has meanwhile assumed the honourable name of *Bristol Queen* and is now based on the inner Bristol Channel.

At various times small craft provided excursions from Rothesay, and in the post-1945 years, one of these was the *Maid of Bute*. Little is known of her history, but she was owned by John Knox and used on cruises to the Kyles of Bute, Loch Striven and Dunoon. She was quite a comfortable little vessel and easily recognisable by her vivid colour scheme; originally she had a bright-green hull with white saloon and yellow funnel, but by 1966 her hull colour had been changed to yellow. She was sold to owners in Fort William in 1973.

One of the most interesting of the smaller craft was the *Countess of Breadalbane* (1936). Built for cruising on Loch Awe, she was transferred by road to the Clyde in 1952 for ferry duties and, after a good deal of initial opposition, became a useful and well-liked member of the fleet, being equally at home on the Largs–Millport ferry, late-evening sailings or charter work. From 1967 to 1971 she was the regular Holy Loch ship. In 1971 she was sold to Mr Ritchie of Gourock to replace the *Gourockian* and, as it was a condition of sale that her name be changed, became the *Countess of Kempock*. After a later charter for sailings in the Iona area, she went to Loch Lomond.

The *Ashton* alongside Largs Pier on 23 June 1952. Behind, to the left of the church, can be seen the art-deco façade of Nardini's restaurant and ice-cream parlour, without a visit to which establishment no day trip to Largs was or (happily) is complete.
G. A. Osbon, courtesy of the World Ship Society

The *Countess of Breadalbane* at Gourock in 1975 after renaming as the *Countess of Kempock*. Author

In 1965 the *Ashton* was sold to Mr R. Ritchie of Gourock for local ferry services and, as can be seen in this view taken there in June 1967, acquired a dark-blue hull. *T. J. Edgington*

After 1945, only cruises to Rothesay from Ireland were maintained by ships of the Isle of Man Steam Packet Co. On a July evening in 1960 the *Snaefell* has ousted the *Waverley* from Berth 1, her usual departure point for the last run to Craigendoran. *Author*

The *Maid of Bute* was one of a number of smaller craft to provide excursions from Rothesay postwar. By the time this photograph was taken in 1966 her hull had been painted yellow. *T. J. Edgington*

From *c*1900 occasional excursions were given from Clyde piers to Bangor or Belfast by the mail ships of G. & J. Burns. These excursions lapsed during and after World War 1 but were revived between 1932 and 1939. Sometimes the sailings were taken by 'one of the larger mail steamers' (according to Burns' publicity), but this view shows the Ardrossan–Belfast daylight-service paddle steamer *Adder* off King's Cross, Arran, on one such cruise. *Author's collection*

No visitor to the Clyde in the 'glory days' could have failed to notice the 'puffers' going about their business, since they were as much part of the scene as any of the passenger steamers. Here the *Boer* heads upriver near Erskine in July 1961. She had been built in 1941 and had, with her fleet-mate *Inca*, played a role in the film *The Maggie*. Both were scrapped in 1965. *G. A. Osbon, courtesy of the World Ship Society*

13. PLEASURE STEAMERS WITH A DIFFERENCE

The Clyde sewage-purification scheme executed by Glasgow Corporation between 1894 and 1904 has already been mentioned, and in the latter year, the first sludge boat was acquired. After World War 1, convalescent soldiers were given free outings on the Corporation's vessels, and from 1925 this practice was developed considerably. The *Dalmarnock* of 1925 had accommodation for 70 passengers, with a comfortable saloon and dining saloon; the *Shieldhall* of 1955 — the last passenger steamer to be built for service on the Firth — could carry 80. The trips, for organised groups only, were free and gave the opportunity of a day out on the Firth to many who would not have been able to afford the fare for the railway steamers, thousands being carried over the years. Despite their lowly calling, the sludge boats were always kept in immaculate condition, in an attractive colour scheme of grey hull, brown upperworks and a yellow funnel.

PASSENGERS AND CREW

Watched by a couple of children, the crew of the *Kenilworth* pose for a photograph at Craigendoran in 1914. By this date the employment of stewardesses was regular practice, the first recorded being aboard the *Lady Rowena* in 1891. Until well after World War 2, many deck hands and not a few officers on Clyde steamers were Gaelic-speakers, but, even on MacBrayne ships, the language had no official standing on the Firth. *McLean Museum & Art Gallery*

Captain James Williamson (back row, right) and crew members of the *Viceroy* in the late 1870s. The Williamson house flag — a blue pennant with a yellow star and crescent — adorns the jerseys of some of the crew, but many wear no uniform at all. *McLean Museum & Art Gallery*

A scene on the upper deck of the *Duchess of Hamilton* on 27 August 1967. Headscarves were always popular on board, but by this date the anorak had also begun to make an appearance.
T. J. Edgington

In contrast with the picture on the far left, the passengers (including children) on the after deck of the *Ivanhoe* are dressed in the height of Edwardian fashion, and everyone is wearing a hat.
Author's collection

Passengers on board the *Maid of Skelmorlie* c1970. The lack of deck space is readily apparent.
Dr Alastair C. Harper

14. BRITISH RAILWAYS MODERNISATION — FOUR LITTLE MAIDS AND CAR FERRIES

By 1950 it was clear that something would have to be done to reduce the losses being incurred in the running of the Clyde services and also to revitalise the fleet, and in February 1951 a £1 million modernisation plan was announced. Part of this plan provided for the building of four passenger motor ships for shuttle services between the main piers. Unfortunately their construction coincided with a singularly cack-handed attempt to close certain small piers; as a result of the opposition to this, the shuttle plan was dropped and the new vessels were used on conventional services. All were identical, although construction was shared between three yards and all entered service in June and July 1953.

The 'Maids', as the four new ships were known, were economical and highly manoeuvrable little vessels, and, although they could roll, they were good sea-boats. But perhaps because of the change of plan when they were already under construction, they were not quite right for any of the uses to which they were put. Deck space was inadequate, and when used on cruising they became unpleasantly crowded with anything over 100 passengers on board. The fore saloon, with

After conversion to a car ferry and in Caledonian MacBrayne colours, the *Maid of Cumbrae* leaves Gourock for Dunoon in May 1973. *Author*

its rows of bus-type seats, was not the best place for sightseeing, and only a hardened drinker would linger in the dark little bar below! On the other hand, they were still too large for commuter runs in winter. With hindsight, it would have been better to have built only three vessels — a small 200-passenger ferry for the Holy Loch, a shuttle ferry and one slightly larger for cruising, on the lines of the *Balmoral*.

The CSP used them to inaugurate an imaginative range of shorter cruises, including 'café' cruises, the fare of 3s 6d including a cup of coffee and a chocolate (Penguin) biscuit.

The first three 'Maids' were sold off in 1973/4, but the *Maid of Cumbrae*, converted to become a car ferry, lasted until 1978. Ironically, both she and the *Maid of Skelmorlie* (which also became a car ferry) seem to have been much more successful in the Gulf of Naples than they were on the Clyde, both being still in service at the time of writing, as the *Capri Express* and the *Ala* respectively.

The other part of the 1951 modernisation plan was the construction of what were called 'general purpose' ships, intended primarily for use as car ferries but also given space and handling equipment for general cargo. Named *Arran*, *Bute* and *Cowal*, they were often referred to as the 'ABCs'. Passenger facilities were somewhat basic, but as car ferries they proved to be brilliantly successful, to the extent that they were inadequate for the traffic offering by the mid-1960s. The cargo capacity was not used as such to any extent, and in 1958/9 they were rearranged to give additional car space, allowing them to carry

36 cars of average size, rather than the original 24. The *Arran* was converted to drive-on/off layout in 1973 and was latterly used frequently on services in West Highland waters, having been transferred to David MacBrayne in 1970. The others remained in their original condition, although the *Bute* also migrated to the Hebrides from 1973 onwards. All were withdrawn in the late 1970s, and, although sold to other owners, none saw further service.

It had been intended that one of the 'ABCs' would serve Arran, but demand on the upper Firth was such that this was impossible, and in 1957 a further ship was launched for the Arran run. Named *Glen Sannox*, she had vastly improved passenger accommodation, good deck space and an hydraulic car hoist, allowing the carriage of heavier loads than on the 'ABCs'. After 1971 she was used on other routes, including those in the Hebrides and, with less success, was also used as a cruise ship from 1978. She was finally sold out of the fleet in 1989, after a most useful career, and was then used in service in the Red Sea.

'CAFE' CRUISE 'CAFE' CRUISE
Rothesay Pier
and
CRUISE
CHARGE 3/6
(H)
For conditions see over

TEA or COFFEE
(Rothesay Pier)
This portion to be handed to the Steward
(H)
For conditions see over

The mini-skirted girl on the right and the bearded crew member with the luggage barrow on the left indicate the arrival of the 1970s, as a Triumph Herald is driven aboard the *Glen Sannox* at Rothesay in August 1970.
T. J. Edgington

The *Glen Sannox* arriving at Ardrossan's Winton Pier in July 1967. *Author*

▼ In May 1965 the *Maid of Ashton* shows off her monastral-blue hullas she leaves Gourock on a commuter run to the Holy Loch. *Author*

▲ The *Cowal* coming alongside Rothesay Pier in June 1973. She is still in CSP livery, and the traditional gangway in the foreground recalls the old order. *Author*

15. REVOLUTION

◄ Just before the CSP takeover, the *Dhuirnish* waits at the Rhubodach slip in August 1969. *T. J. Edgington*

Just before World War 2 the CSP had shown interest in the question of a car-ferry service across the Narrows of the Kyles of Bute, between Colintraive and Rhubodach. However, the war intervened, and it was left to private enterprise, in the form of the Bute Ferry Co, to begin such a service, on 13 July 1950 — a date which marked the beginning of a revolution in Clyde services. At first, converted landing craft were used, but in 1963 a purpose-built ferry, the *Eilean Bhuide,* appeared, being supplemented in 1967 by the *Dhuirnish,* a turntable ferry which was then converted to bow-loading. As the names of both ships were mis-spelled, it would seem that Gaelic was not a strong point with the BFC! In 1965 the monthly return fare for a car of up to 1,500cc was 15s — considerably less than on the CSP ships, on which a Wemyss Bay–Rothesay return was from 36s upwards — and the service prospered.

On 31 December 1969 the service was taken over by the CSP, and in 1970/1 two ex-Skye ferries replaced the *Eilean Bhuide* and the *Dhuirnish.*

The 1960s began with a run of poor summers and by the middle of the decade it was clear that Clyde services could not long continue on their traditional lines. On 1 January 1969, following the Transport Act of 1968, the CSP passed out of railway control after 80 years and became part of the new Scottish Transport Group. Exactly four years later it was merged with MacBraynes as Caledonian MacBrayne Ltd. The years which followed saw revolution as great as that set in train by John and Alexander Williamson 80 years before. Credit for the speed and smoothness of the transition, which took place in an incredibly short space of time, was in large measure due to James Kirkwood and John Whittle, who came

The *Caledonia* at Ardrossan in June 1970, just one month after entering service. *Author*

Hovercraft HM2-011 approaches Dunoon in August 1970. *T. J. Edgington*

▲
A photograph taken from
the upper deck of the *Waverley,*
showing the *Iona* loading
at Gourock in June 1971.
Author

SUMMER SAIL 72

Services & Excursions

27th MAY UNTIL 30th SEPTEMBER

Caledonian Steam Packet

INCLUDING RAIL CONNECTIONS FROM GLASGOW

▲
The last CSP
summer timetable,
1972.

from the Scottish Bus Group in 1969 and 1970 to become Secretary and Manager respectively of the CSP and (after 1973) Caledonian MacBrayne.

Caledonia (1970)

Passengers on the Clyde did not have to wait long for the first ▼ sign of change. The Scottish Transport Group wanted to modernise its operations as quickly as possible and for the Ardrossan–Arran service bought the four-year-old car ferry *Stena Baltica,* which had been running from Tilbury to Calais. Renamed *Caledonia,* she took up service on 29 May 1970, in full CSP livery. However, this decision was perhaps taken too quickly: although furnished to a standard not previously seen on any Clyde car ferry, the *Caledonia* had a distressing tendency to roll in even a moderate sea, and her speed of 14 knots was too slow for the service. Moreover, as her passenger capacity was only 650 in summer and an incredibly low 132 in winter, it was necessary to institute sailing tickets on winter weekends. Arran residents and visitors were not impressed! She was replaced on the summer service by the *Clansman* in 1976 but remained on the winter run until 1984. She was finally sold out of the fleet in December 1987.

Iona (1970)

MacBrayne had in December 1968 ordered a new ship for the Islay service from the Ailsa shipyard at Troon, but in the event this ship, named *Iona,* went into service on the Gourock–Dunoon route on 29 May 1970, her rather absurd little funnel being painted in CSP colours. She was the first drive-through ship to operate on the route, and her passenger facilities were of a far higher standard than those of the earlier 'ABC' ferries. In July 1971 she opened the linkspans at her two terminal piers, and the 'roll-on, roll-off' era was inaugurated. She did not remain long on the Clyde thereafter, as she was moved to West Highland services, though she occasionally returned as a relief ship. She is now employed in the Orkneys by another operator. Wherever the *Iona* went, she was a success.

HM2-011

The new administration was also keen to try out new forms of water transport, and in 1970 a side-wall hovercraft was placed in service between Gourock, Dunoon, Rothesay, Largs and Millport. She was quite successful in operation and was much quieter than the other hovercraft which were tried, but lasted only two seasons on the Firth.

Largs

One of the first actions of the new management was to institute, on 11 March 1972, a ferry service between Largs and a slip on the island of Cumbrae. To cater for this two redundant

The timetable for *Highland Seabird*, for her Clyde sailings in 1976.

	FROM ROTHESAY AND DUNOON									TO ROTHESAY AND DUNOON		
MONDAYS TO FRIDAYS										**MONDAYS TO FRIDAYS**		
				BRITISH RAIL CONNECTIONS								
R'say depart	Dunoon depart	H'burgh arrive	G'nock arrive	depart G'nock	arrive Glgw	depart Glgw	arrive G'nock	G'nock depart	H'burgh depart	Dunoon arrive	R'say arrive
0710ᶜ	0740ᶜ		0758	0810	0843	0720	0801	0810ᶜ		0826	
	0840ᵉ		0856	0913	0958	0820	0901	0910	0930ᵀ	0948	1020
1030	1105		1121	1133	1218	1025	1106	1130		1149	1222
1230	1305	1323ᵀ	1344	1353	1429	1305	1346	1355		1412	1445
1530	1605		1627	1653	1729	1555	1629	1640ᶜ		1656	
	1705ᵉ		1723	1733	1818	1655	1729	1740ᶜ		1756	1830
1845	1920	1938ᵀ	2000	2013	2058	1925	2006	2015		2031	
	2040		2100	2113	2158	2005	2046	2110		2128	2200

SATURDAYS										**SATURDAYS**		
0815	0845		0901	0913	0958	0820	0901	0910	0930ᵀ	0950	1020
1030	1100	Sailing to Glasgow		arr. 1230		1245 dep.	Sailing from Glasgow			1415	1445
1530	1600	Sailing to Glasgow		arr. 1730		1745 dep.	Sailing from Glasgow			1915	1945
2000	2030	2050ᵀ	2110	2133	2218	2025	2106	2120		2136	2215

SUNDAYS									**SUNDAYS**	
0945	1015	Sailing to Glasgow	arr. 1145	1945 dep.	Sailing from Glasgow				2115	2145

SUNDAY CRUISE
KYLES OF BUTE AND LOCH FYNE

Glasgow depart	Dunoon arrive	Dunoon depart	R'say arrive	R'say depart	T'bert arrive	T'bert depart	R'say arrive	R'say depart	Dunoon arrive	Dunoon depart	Glasgow arrive
1200	1325	1335	1400	1430	1530	1625	1720	1730	1755	1805	1930

C: Commuter Sailings — Restricted Ten Journey Tickets are valid on these sailings only.

T: These sailings are subject to tidal conditions at Helensburgh. For up to date information see notice boards at

ferries were transferred from the Kyle of Lochalsh–Kyleakin service and converted to bow loading at Troon. One was the *Kyleakin II* (the numeral having been added in 1970), which was renamed *Largs*.

Jupiter (Gaelic Iupadar) (1973)

While the first two new, large ships to appear on the Clyde had been in the nature of stop-gaps, the management of what had on 1 January 1973 become Caledonian MacBrayne was determined to provide new purpose-built car ferries, and the first of these entered service on the Gourock–Dunoon route on 18 March 1974. Although her design owed something to Western Ferries' *Sound of Islay*, the new ship has comfortable accommodation for 650 passengers, as well as a car capacity

of 40. Voith-Schneider propellers allow her to turn in her own length and a bow thrust unit allows her to move sideways from a pier. With other members of the fleet, she acquired the Gaelic version of her name in 2002.

Sound of Scarba, Sound of Shuna

Competition returned to the Clyde with the opening of Western Ferries' McKinlay's Point–Hunter's Quay service in 1973. The service was worked initially by two former Swedish ferries — the *Sound of Scarba* (ex-*Olandsund III*) and the *Sound of Shuna* (ex-*Olandsund IV*) — which were functional to the point of austerity. Despite the total absence of passenger accommodation, the service scored on grounds of convenience and frequency. There was soon a need for larger ships, with a reasonable

The *Largs* seen with the *Keppel*, which had been brought from the Thames in 1967 to operate the Largs–Millport passenger ferry and was previously the Tilbury–Gravesend ferry *Rose*. Robert Grieves

When built, the *Jupiter* lacked the flying bridge fitted to her later sister *Juno*, but one was added during her first winter overhaul, in 1975. In her first year the bulwarks around her car deck were also painted white, an attractive feature which did not last. As built, she pulls away from Gourock in May 1974. *Author*

The *Sound of Scarba* (ex-*Olandsund III*) seen off McKinlay's Point in 1982. *Author*

▲ The *Queen of Scots* alongside Rothesay Pier in 1975, still with her former name of *Bournemouth Queen*. *Author*

▲ The *Highland Seabird* approaches Dunoon in June 1976. The next catamaran to operate on the Clyde would be the *Ali Cat*, used on the Gourock–Dunoon passenger runs in the winter of 2002/3. *Author*

◀ The *Pioneer* has recently become closely identified with the Clyde and is seen here at Dunoon, helping with Cowal Games traffic. *Author*

amount of covered saloon seating, but the two pioneers nevertheless had long careers on the Clyde, the *Sound of Shuna* lasting until 2001.

Queen of Scots

In the mid-1970s oil-rig construction at a site in Ardyne (opposite Rothesay) was in full swing, and, to transport workers, owner MacAlpine bought an attractive little motor ship which had started life as the *Coronia* at Scarborough in 1938. Having arrived as the *Bournemouth Queen*, she was soon renamed as the *Queen of Scots* and also provided some public cruises.

Highland Seabird

In 1976 Western Ferries experimented with a Norwegian-built catamaran. This vessel was chartered for five months as the *Highland Seabird* and during that period ran services between Greenock, Helensburgh, Dunoon and Rothesay, with longer cruises at weekends. Upriver trips to Glasgow were also briefly tried but were abandoned due to problems posed by driftwood. The service was successful but was not repeated in any further year, and for the remainder of her time in Scotland the craft operated in West Highland waters.

Pioneer (Gaelic *Teoraiche*)

The first new-building programme of Caledonian MacBrayne was completed with the delivery of the *Pioneer* from the Leith yard of Robb Caledon in 1974. She was the first ship of the fleet designed to serve equally on services of both the constituent companies and in fact spent most of her early years in West Highland waters. While she lacks the graceful lines of early steamers, she nevertheless has a purposeful air about her, and at speed she can produce a most impressive bow wave. She has served on most routes of Caledonian MacBrayne and must be counted a most versatile and useful member of the fleet.

Management which was concerned with change and modernisation also showed a remarkable awareness of its heritage, and one of the most significant events of this period was the decision to present the *Waverley* to the Paddle Steamer Preservation Society when it was decided that her days of commercial sailing were over, in 1973.

16. THE CLYDE IN 1977

By 1977 the revolution was over and the Clyde services had settled in to their new pattern. Dunoon, with a half-hourly frequency provided by the *Juno* and *Jupiter*, and Rothesay, with eight sailings per day (Monday-Friday) by the *Glen Sannox*, enjoyed a level of service that people a century earlier could only have dreamed of. A new ship was on order for the Rothesay station. The Largs–Cumbrae ferries shuttled back and forth every half hour, and already it had proved necessary to introduce a new and larger ferry — the *Isle of Cumbrae* of 1976 — on this crossing. These were supplemented by eight direct sailings by the *Keppel*. On the Arran station the *Clansman* provided a basic service of five sailings in each direction per day, though the best through Glasgow–Brodick timing was 121 minutes — a far cry from the 80 minutes of 1892. With the conversion of the Wemyss Bay–Rothesay service, all main routes were now drive-through, the *Arran* acting as spare ship. Small ferries provided links between Rhubodach and Colintraive and between Lochranza and Claonaig, and, as connections were provided by local buses, not only car drivers benefited. But the small piers had almost vanished from the scene — only Kilcreggan received a regular service, while Tighnabruaich and Tarbert had only excursion calls. Western Ferries kept Hunter's Quay busier than it ever had been. Attempts to run fast ferries had been abandoned, and all main services were worked by ships which provided under-cover accommodation for all passengers, even if this was in some cases rather basic. The Caledonian MacBrayne services required five large ferries and one large pleasure steamer, five small ferries and one small passenger ship — 12 vessels in all. Competition had returned to the Firth, Western Ferries having three ships in commission, and there were two other excursion ships — the *Waverley* and the *Queen of Scots*. In all, 17 vessels did the work done by 35 a century earlier. Exact comparison of passenger numbers is impossible, since figures do not exist for the early days, but in 1977 they probably carried more passengers and certainly more cars!

For the cruises of what was once again the *Queen Mary* Caledonian MacBrayne produced one of the most elegant pieces of publicity ever to advertise a Clyde steamer — a silver brochure to mark also the year of HM Queen Elizabeth's Silver Jubilee. But the range of cruises was now considerably reduced — old favourites such as Arran via Kyles of Bute were still visited frequently, but Campbeltown featured only occasionally and Inveraray not at all. The fare from Glasgow to Brodick was now £7.21, though discounts for advance purchase and also family tickets were available; in 1914 it had been 4s by Third-class rail and Saloon on steamer. In both years, this was probably about 10% of a skilled workman's weekly wage; the figures had altered, the level of fares hardly at all. Sadly, despite the excellent publicity, this was the *Queen Mary*'s last year in Clyde service, cruises thereafter being handed over, with poor results, to the *Glen Sannox*.

And then there was the *Waverley*. She was by now into her third summer of preservation with the Waverley Steam Navigation Co and was proving successful. This was also the first in which she ventured outwith the Clyde area, to the Mersey. It was also to be a bad year for the paddler, which had her second argument with the Gantocks off Dunoon on 15 July, and she had to be withdrawn. Fortunately the little *Queen of Scots* was now available for charter and, repainted in traditional LNER colours, she managed to carry 14,000 passengers in the remainder of the Clyde season and thus minimised the losses for the WSNC. And so, a century after the first *Lord of the Isles*, the Clyde gained another pleasure steamer!

Take a Jubilee Year Cruise aboard "Queen Mary"

Britain's finest Pleasure Steamer

Day Cruises on the Firth of Clyde

Caledonian MacBrayne

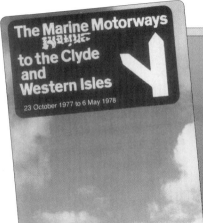

The Winter 1977/8 timetable, depicting the *Caledonia* heading out from Gourock into an appropriately choppy sea.

▲
In her final condition, the *Queen Mary* draws into Dunoon Pier on a tranquil summer's evening. She is still majestic, but the shortening of the masts has ruined her profile.
Dr Alastair C. Harper

The *Queen of Scots* in Waverley Steam Navigation Co colours at Glasgow in November 1977. *Author*

▲

The *Saturn* approaching Rothesay on a January morning in 1987. *Author*

New ships of 1977

▼ Built by the Ailsa Ship Building Co, the *Saturn* (Gaelic *Satharn*)
was basically a repeat of the earlier ferries, but her upper deck
extends around the superstructure and her bridge is one level
higher. Although launched in June 1977, technical problems
delayed this ship's entry into service until February 1978,
whereupon the revolution in Clyde services was complete.
In just nine years, Caledonian MacBrayne, under the
energetic management of John Whittle, had brought about a
change as great as that wrought by the Caledonian and GSW
railways 80 years earlier.

The Clyde also gained a new cruise ship in 1977, albeit in
the guise of the latest and (as matters turned out) the last
of the Glasgow sludge boats. The *Garroch Head* was built in
1977 by James Lamont of Port Glasgow for what had by
then become Strathclyde Regional Council and had
accommodation for 70 passengers. She made the last
sailing with passengers on 24 September 1998 and closed
the service on 31 December of that year, new regulations
having made it impossible to continue dumping waste
material at sea. With her went not only a tradition of public
service but also the regular use of Gaelic by the crew of a
ship on the Firth.

17. THE WAVERLEY

In 1974, for the first time since 1812, no paddle steamer sailed the waters of the Clyde, but the efforts of enthusiasts and inspired action by the management of Caledonian MacBrayne ensured that the beat of paddles had not disappeared for ever from the Firth, and in the following year, the *Waverley* was able to re-enter service. Let the accompanying pictures serve as a tribute to the ship and to all those who through her have kept alive the traditions of the Clyde steamers into the 21st century. Rejuvenated by a major rebuilding in 2000, completed by further work in the winter of 2002/3, she can now look forward to maintaining this tradition of the glory days for many years to come.

▲ It is hard now to remember that in her early days the *Waverley* had to take her turn on year-round ferry services; as such she is seen about to leave Gourock for Dunoon on a winter's day in late 1953. There appear to be more crew than passengers!
Author

◄ The *Waverley* sailing across Rothesay Bay in LNER colours in 1947.
Author's collection

Alongside her home base at Craigendoran in September 1967, the *Waverley* displays her blue hull, with red lions rampant on her funnels. This was the CSP version of British Rail's corporate livery.
B. A. Jenkins

In 1973, her last year in commercial service, the *Waverley* acquired the new Caledonian MacBrayne red funnels. She is seen calling at Tarbert on 1 June of that year.
Author

Proudly flying the house flag of the Waverley Steam Navigation Co, the *Waverley* hurries away from Rothesay.
Author

In James Watt Dock, Greenock, in August 1974, Douglas McGowan of the Waverley Steam Navigation Co hands over a Royal Bank of Scotland £1 note to Sir Patrick Thomas, Chairman of the Scottish Transport Group. (The £1 note had actually been donated by Sir Patrick!) John Whittle, Manager of Caledonian MacBrayne (right), and Terry Sylvester of the WSNC (left) witness the passing of the ship into preservation.
Douglas McGowan collection

BIBLIOGRAPHY

There is now a vast range of literature on Clyde steamers, and a complete résumé is beyond the scope of this book. The following have been used in its preparation:

Brown, A.: *Craigendoran Steamers* (Aggregate Publications, Johnstone, 1979);

Chisholm, A.: *Millport Pier Album* (St Maura Press, 1992);

Clark, A. J. C.: *Caley to the Coast* (Oakwood Press, Usk, Monmouthshire, 2001);

Duckworth, C. L. D., and Langmuir, G. E.: *Clyde River and Other Steamers*, 4th edition (Brown, Son & Ferguson Ltd, Glasgow, 1990);

Inglis, J. C. A.: *Brodick–Arran in the Great War, 1914-1918*;

Lyon, D. J. (ed): *The Denny List* (National Maritime Museum, Greenwich, 1975);

MacArthur, I. C.: *The Caledonian Steam Packet Company* (Clyde River Steamer Club, Glasgow, 1971);

McCrorie, I., and Monteith, J.: *Clyde Piers — A Pictorial Record* (Inverclyde District Libraries, Greenock, 1981);

McCrorie, I.: *Dunoon Pier — A Celebration* (Argyll Publishing, Glendaruel, Argyll, 1997);

McCrorie, I. C.: *Royal Road to the Isles* (Caledonian MacBrayne Ltd, Gourock, 2001);

Maclagan, I.: *The Piers and Ferries of Bute* (Buteshire Natural History Society, Rothesay, 1997);

McQueen, A.: *Clyde River Steamers of the last Fifty Years* (Gowans & Gray, Glasgow, 1923);

McQueen, A.: *Echoes of Old Clyde Paddle Wheels* (Gowans & Gray, Glasgow, 1924);

Meek, D.: *An t-Aiseag an Iar* (Pollock & Co, Greenock, 1977);

Moir, P., and Crawford, I.: *Clyde Shipwrecks* (M. Crawford, Wemyss Bay, 1988);

Paterson, A. J. S.: *The Golden Years of the Clyde Steamers (1889-1914)* (David & Charles, Newton Abbot, 1969);

Paterson, A. J. S.: *The Victorian Summer of the Clyde Steamers (1864-1888)* (David & Charles, Newton Abbot, 1972);

Quinn, I., Robertson, D., and Stevenson, D.: *From Dalmuir to Garroch Head — The Story of Sludge Disposal Ships on the Clyde* (West of Scotland Water, Glasgow, 2001);

Smith, C. J.: *In Fair Weather and Foul — 30 Years of Scottish Passenger Ships and Ferries* (Ferry Publications, Narberth, Pembrokeshire, 1999);

Rankin, Stuart W. (editor), *Sou' West Journal No 33* (Glasgow & South Western Railway Association, 2001)

Walker, F. A., and Sinclair, F.: *North Clyde Estuary — An Architectural Guide* (Royal Incorporation of Architects in Scotland, Edinburgh, 1992);

Whittle, J.: *Speed, Bonny Boat — Caledonian MacBrayne 1969-1990* (Saltire Communications, Edinburgh, 1990);

Williamson, Captain James: *Clyde Passenger Steamers, 1812-1901*, facsimile edition (Spa Books, Stevenage, 1987);

(various authors): *Waverley — The Golden Jubilee* (A. T. Condie, Nuneaton, and Waverley Excursions Ltd, Glasgow, 1997);

Minutes of the Boards of the Caledonian Steam Packet Co, the North British Steam Packet Co and the Steam Vessels Sub-committees of the Glasgow & South Western Railway and the London, Midland & Scottish Railway;

Newspaper articles in the *Glasgow Herald*, the *Evening Times*, the *Oban Times* and the *Ardrossan & Saltcoats Herald*;

Timetables of Caledonian, GSWR, LNER, LMS and Williamson-Buchanan steamers;

Guidebooks of David MacBrayne, 1905 season, and various timetables.

The following organisations may be of interest to those who wish to learn more about the steamers and the railway companies which operated them (addresses current as at 2003):

Clyde River Steamer Club (S. Craig, 50 Earlspark Avenue, Newlands, Glasgow G43 2HW);

Glasgow & South Western Railway Association (G. Robinson, 4 Clochoderick Avenue, Kilbarchan, Renfrewshire, PA10 2AY);

Caledonian Railway Association (F. Landery, 45 Sycamore Drive, Hamilton, Lanarkshire, ML3 7HF).